Evaluating Research in Academic Journals

A Practical Guide to Realistic Evaluation

SIXTH EDITION

Fred Pyrczak

LONDON AND NEW YORK

First published 1999 by Pyrczak Publishing.

Published 2017 by Routledge
2 Park Square, Milton Park, Abingdon, Oxon OX14 4RN
711 Third Avenue, New York, NY 10017, USA

Routledge is an imprint of the Taylor & Francis Group, an informa business

This edition was written in collaboration with Randall R. Bruce.

Cover design by Ruben Hornillo.

ISBN-13: 978-1-936-52334-4 (pbk)

Contents

Notes

Introduction to the Sixth Edition

When students in the social and behavioral sciences take advanced courses in their major field of study, they are often required to read and evaluate original research reports published as articles in academic journals. This book is designed as a guide for students who are first learning how to engage in this process.

Major Assumptions

First, it is assumed that the students using this book have limited knowledge of research methods, even though they may have taken a course in introductory research methods (or may be using this book while taking such a course). Because of this assumption, technical terms and jargon such as *true experiment* are defined when they are first used in this book.

Second, it is assumed that students have only a limited grasp of elementary statistics. Thus, the chapters on evaluating statistical reporting in research reports are confined to criteria that such students can easily comprehend.

Finally, and perhaps most important, it is assumed that students with limited backgrounds in research methods and statistics can produce adequate evaluations of research reports—evaluations that get to the heart of important issues and allow students to draw sound conclusions from published research.

This Book Is *Not* Written for...

This book is not written for journal editors or members of their editorial review boards. Such professionals usually have had firsthand experience in conducting research and have taken advanced courses in research methods and statistics. Published evaluation criteria for use by these professionals are often terse, full of jargon, and composed of many elements that cannot be fully comprehended without advanced training and experience. This book is aimed at a completely different audience: students who are just beginning to learn how to evaluate original reports of research published in journals.

Applying the Evaluation Questions in This Book

Chapters 2 through 13 are organized around evaluation questions that may be answered with a simple "yes" or "no," where a "yes" indicates that students judge a characteristic to be satisfactory. However, for evaluation questions that deal with complex issues, students may also want to rate each one using a scale from 1 to 5, where 5 is the highest rating. In addition, N/A (not applicable) may be used when students believe a characteristic does not apply, and I/I (insufficient information) may be used if the research report does not contain sufficient information for an informed judgment to be made.

Evaluating Quantitative and Qualitative Research

Quantitative and qualitative research differ in purpose as well as methodology. Students who are not familiar with the distinctions between the two approaches are advised to read Appendix A, which presents a very brief overview of the differences, and Appendix B, which provides an overview of important issues in the evaluation of qualitative research.

Note From the Author

My best wishes are with you as you master the art and science of evaluating research. With the aid of this book, you should find the process both undaunting and fascinating as you seek defensible conclusions regarding research on topics that interest you.

Fred Pyrczak
Los Angeles

Chapter 1

Background for Evaluating Research Reports

The vast majority of research reports are initially published in academic journals. In these reports, researchers describe how they identified a research problem, made relevant observations to gather data, and analyzed the data they collected. The reports usually conclude with a discussion of the results and their implications. This chapter provides an overview of some general characteristics of such research. Subsequent chapters present specific questions that should be applied in the evaluation of research reports.

✓ Guideline 1: Researchers often examine narrowly defined problems.

Comment: While researchers usually are interested in broad problem areas, they very often examine only narrow aspects of the problems because of limited resources and the desire to keep the research manageable by limiting its focus. Furthermore, they often examine problems in such a way that the results can be easily reduced to statistics, further limiting the breadth of their research.[1]

Example 1.1.1 briefly describes a study on two correlates of prosocial behavior (i.e., helping behavior). To make the study of this issue manageable, the researchers greatly limited its scope. Specifically, they examined only one very narrow type of prosocial behavior (making donations to homeless men who were begging in public).

Example 1.1.1

A study on prosocial behavior, narrowly defined:

In order to study the relationship between prosocial behavior and gender as well as age, researchers located five men who appeared to be homeless and were soliciting money on street corners using cardboard signs. Without approaching the men, the researchers observed them from a short distance for two hours each. For each pedestrian who walked within ten feet of the men, the researchers recorded whether the pedestrian made a donation. The researchers also recorded the gender and approximate age of each pedestrian.

Because researchers often conduct their research on narrowly defined problems, an important task in the evaluation of research is to judge whether a researcher has

[1] Qualitative researchers (see Appendices A and B) generally take a broader view when defining a problem to be explored in research and are not constrained by the need to reduce the results to numbers and statistics.

defined the problem so narrowly that it fails to make an important contribution to the advancement of knowledge.

✓ Guideline 2: Researchers often conduct studies in artificial settings.

Comment: Laboratories on university campuses are often the settings for research. To study the effects of alcohol consumption on driving behavior, a group of participants might be asked to drink carefully measured amounts of alcohol in a laboratory and then "drive" using virtual-reality simulators. Example 1.2.1 describes the preparation of the cocktails in a study of this type.

Example 1.2.1[2]

Alcoholic beverages prepared for consumption in a laboratory setting:

The preparation of the cocktail was done in a separate area out of view of the participant. All cocktails were a 16-oz mixture of orange juice, cranberry juice, grapefruit juice (ratio 4:2:1, respectively). For the cocktails containing alcohol, we added 2 oz of 190-proof grain alcohol mixed thoroughly. For the placebo cocktail, we lightly sprayed the surface of the juice cocktail with alcohol using an atomizer placed slightly above the juice surface to impart an aroma of alcohol to the glass and beverage surface. This placebo cocktail was then immediately given to the participant to consume. This procedure results in the same alcohol aroma being imparted to the placebo cocktail as the alcohol cocktail....

Such a study might have limited generalizability to drinking in out-of-laboratory settings, such as nightclubs, the home, picnics, and other places where those who are consuming alcohol may be drinking different amounts at different rates while consuming (or not consuming) various foods. Nevertheless, conducting such research in a laboratory allows researchers to simplify and control variables such as the amount of alcohol consumed, the types of food being consumed, the number of individuals in a car, and so on. In short, researchers very often opt against studying variables in complex, real-life settings for the more interpretable research results typically obtained in a laboratory.

✓ Guideline 3: Researchers use less-than-perfect methods of observation.

Comment: In research, *observation* can take many forms—from paper-and-pencil multiple-choice achievement tests to essay examinations, from administering a paper-and-pencil attitude scale with choices from "strongly agree" to "strongly disagree" to conducting unstructured interviews to identify interviewees' attitudes.[3] Of

---

[2] Barkley, R. A., Murphy, K. R., O'Connell, T., Anderson, D., & Connor, D. F. (2006). Effects of two doses of alcohol on simulator driving performance in adults with attention-deficit/hyperactivity disorder. *Neuropsychology*, *20*, 77–87.

[3] Researchers sometimes refer to measurement tools for making observations as *instruments*, especially in older literature.

course, *observation* also includes direct observation of individuals interacting in either their natural environments or laboratory settings.

It is safe to assume that all methods of observation are flawed to some extent. To see why this is so, consider a professor/researcher who is interested in studying racial relations in society in general. Because of limited resources, the researcher decides to make direct observations of White and African American students interacting (and/or not interacting) in the college cafeteria. The observations will necessarily be limited to the types of behaviors typically exhibited in cafeteria settings—a weakness in the researcher's method of observation. In addition, observations will be limited to certain overt behaviors because, for instance, it will be difficult for the researcher to hear most of what is being said without obtruding on the privacy of the students.

On the other hand, suppose that another researcher decides to measure racial attitudes by having students respond anonymously to racial statements by circling "agree" or "disagree" for each one. This researcher has an entirely different set of weaknesses in the observational method. First is the matter of whether students will reveal their real attitudes on such a scale—even if the response is anonymous—because most college students are aware that negative racial attitudes are severely frowned on in academic communities. Thus, some students might indicate what they believe to be socially desirable (i.e., socially "correct") rather than reveal their true attitudes.

In short, *there is no perfect way to measure complex variables*. Instead of expecting perfection, a consumer of research should consider this question: *Is the method sufficiently valid and reliable to provide potentially useful information*?

Examples 1.3.1 and 1.3.2 show statements from research articles in which the researchers acknowledge limitations in their observational methods.

Example 1.3.1[4]

Researchers' acknowledgment of a limitation of their measures:

In addition, the assessment of marital religious discord was limited to one item. Future research should include a multiple-items scale of marital religious discord and additional types of measures, such as interviews or observational coding, as well as multiple informants.

Example 1.3.2[5]

Researchers' acknowledgment of limitations of self-reports for observation:

Despite these strengths, this study is not without limitations. First, the small sample size decreases.... Fourth, neighborhood danger was measured from mothers' self-reports of the events which occurred in the neighborhood during

[4] Kor, A., Mikulincer, M., & Pirutinsky, S. (2012). Family functioning among returnees to Orthodox Judaism in Israel. *Journal of Family Psychology*, *26*, 149–158.

[5] Callahan, K. L., Scaramella, L. V., Laird, R. D., & Sohr-Preston, S. L. (2011). Neighborhood disadvantage as a moderator of the association between harsh parenting and toddler-aged children's internalizing and externalizing problems. *Journal of Family Psychology*, *25*, 68–76.

the past year. Adding other family member reports of the dangerous events and official police reports would clearly strengthen our measure of neighborhood danger.

Chapter 8 provides more information on evaluating observational methods.

✓ Guideline 4: Researchers use less-than-perfect samples.

Comment: Arguably, the most common sampling flaw in research reported in academic journals is the use of *samples of convenience* (i.e., samples that are readily accessible to the researchers). Most researchers are professors, and professors often use samples of college students—obviously as a matter of convenience. Another common flaw is relying on voluntary responses to mailed surveys, which are often quite low, with some researchers arguing that a response rate of about 40% to 60% or more is acceptable. Other samples are flawed because researchers cannot identify and locate all members of a population (e.g., injection drug users). Without being able to do this, it is impossible to draw a sample that a researcher can reasonably defend as being representative of the population.[6] In addition, researchers often have limited resources, which force them to use small samples, which in turn might produce unreliable results.

Researchers sometimes explicitly acknowledge the limitations of their samples. Examples 1.4.1 through 1.4.3 show portions of such statements from research articles.

Example 1.4.1[7]

Researchers' acknowledgment of limitation of sampling (convenience sample):

The present study suffered from several limitations. First of all, the samples were confined to university undergraduate students and only Chinese and American students. For broader generalizations, further studies could recruit people of various ages and educational and occupational characteristics.

Example 1.4.2[8]

Researchers' acknowledgment of limitation of sampling (low rate of participation):

Data were collected using a random sample of e-mail addresses obtained from the university's registrar's office. The response rate (23%) was lower than desired; however, it is unknown what percentage of the e-mail addresses were valid or were being monitored by the targeted student.

---

[6] Qualitative researchers emphasize selecting a *purposive* sample—one that is likely to yield useful information—rather than a *representative* sample.

[7] Jiang, F., Yue, X. D., & Lu, S. (2011). Different attitudes toward humor between Chinese and American students: Evidence from the Implicit Association Test. *Psychological Reports*, *109*, 99–107.

[8] Cox, J. M., & Bates, S. C. (2011). Referent group proximity, social norms, and context: Alcohol use in a low-use environment. *Journal of American College Health*, *59*, 252–259.

Example 1.4.3[9]

Researcher's acknowledgment of limitation of sampling (limited diversity):

There are a number of limitations to this study. The most significant of them relates to the fact that the study was located within one school and the children studied were primarily from a White, working-class community. There is a need to identify how socially and ethnically diverse groups of children use online virtual worlds.

In Chapters 6 and 7, specific criteria for evaluating samples are explored in detail.

✓ Guideline 5: Even a straightforward analysis of data can produce misleading results.

Comment: Obviously, data-input errors and computational errors are possible sources of errors in results. Some commercial research firms have the data they collect entered independently by two or more data-entry clerks. A computer program checks to see whether the two sets of entries match perfectly—if they do not, the errors must be identified before the analysis can proceed. Unfortunately, taking such care in checking for mechanical errors in entering data is hardly ever mentioned in research reports published in academic journals.

In addition, there are alternative statistical methods for most problems, and different methods can yield different results. (See the first evaluation in Chapter 10 for specific examples regarding the selection of statistics.)

Finally, even a nonstatistical analysis can be problematic. For instance, if two or more researchers review extensive transcripts of unstructured interviews, they might differ in their interpretations of the interviewees' responses. Discrepancies such as these suggest that the results may be flawed or at least subject to different interpretations.

Chapter 10 provides evaluation criteria for quantitative Analysis and Results sections of research reports, while Chapter 11 does the same for qualitative Analysis and Results sections.

✓ Guideline 6: Even a single, isolated flaw in research methods can lead to seriously misleading results.

Comment: A seemingly minor flaw such as a poorly worded question on attitudes might lead to results that are incorrect. Likewise, a treatment that has been misapplied in an experiment might lead to misleading conclusions regarding the effectiveness of the treatment. For this reason, research reports should be detailed, so that consumers

---

[9] Marsh, J. (2011). Young children's literacy practices in a virtual world: Establishing an online interaction order. *Reading Research Quarterly*, *46*, 101–118.

of research can judge whether the research methods were flawed. This leads to the next guideline.

✓ Guideline 7: Research reports often contain many details, which can be very important when evaluating a report.

Comment: The old saying "The devil is in the details" applies here. Students who have relied exclusively on secondary sources for information about their major field of study may be surprised at the level of detail in many research reports, which is typically much greater than is implied in sources such as textbooks and classroom lectures. Example 1.7.1 illustrates the level of detail that can be expected in many research reports published in academic journals. It describes part of an intervention for postal service letter carriers. Note the level of detail, such as (1) the color and size of the hats and (2) the specific brand of sunscreen that was distributed. Such details are useful for helping consumers of research understand exactly the nature of the intervention examined in the study. Such detailed descriptions are also helpful for other researchers who might want to replicate the study in order to confirm the findings.

Example 1.7.1[10]

An excerpt from an article illustrating the level of detail often reported in research reports in academic journals:

Within 2 weeks of the baseline measurement, Project SUNWISE health educators visited intervention stations to give out hats, install and dispense sunscreen, distribute materials that prompted use of solar protective strategies, and deliver the initial educational presentation....The machine-washable dark blue hat was made of Cordura nylon, it had a brim that was 4 inches wide in the front and back and 3 inches wide on the sides, and it had an adjustable cord chin strap. In addition to the initial free hat provided by Project SUNWISE, letter carriers at intervention stations were given discounts on replacement hats by the vendor (Watership Trading Companie, Bellingham, WA).

Locker rooms at intervention stations were stocked with large pump bottles of sunscreen (Coppertone Sport, SPF 30, Schering-Plough HealthCare Products, Inc., Memphis, TN) that were refilled regularly by the research staff. Additionally, letter carriers were given free 12-ounce bottles of the sunscreen, which they could refill with sunscreen from the pump bottles. The decision about which sunscreen to use was made on the basis of formative work that identified a product with a high SPF that had an acceptable fragrance and consistency and minimal rub-off from newsprint onto skin....

Finally, Project SUNWISE health educators delivered 6 brief onsite educational presentations over 2 years. The 5- to 10-minute presentations were modeled after the "stand-up talks" letter carriers regularly participated in; the educators used large flip charts with colorful graphics that were tailored to letter carriers. Key points of the introductory presentation included the amount of UVR carriers are exposed to and UVR as a skin cancer risk factor, a case example of a former carrier who recently had a precancerous growth removed, feasible protection strategies, and specific information about the hats and sunscreen. The themes of subsequent presentations were (1) importance of sun safety, even in winter; (2) sun safety for the eyes; (3) sharing sun safety tips with loved ones; (4) relevance of sun safety to letter carriers of all races/ethnicities; and (5) recap and encouragement to continue practicing sun safety behaviors.

---

[10] Mayer, J. A., Slymen, D. J., Clapp, E. J., Pichon, L. C., Eckhardt, L., Eichenfield, L. F., ... Oh, S. S. (2007). Promoting sun safety among U.S. Postal Service letter carriers: Impact of a 2-year intervention. *American Journal of Public Health, 97*, 559–565.

Having detailed information on what was said and done to participants as well as on how the participants were observed makes it possible to make informed evaluations of research.

✓ Guideline 8: Many reports lack information on matters that are potentially important for evaluating a research article.

Comment: In most journals, research reports of more than 15 pages are rare. Journal space is limited by economics—journals have limited readership and thus a limited paid circulation, and they seldom have advertisers. Given this situation, researchers must judiciously choose the details they will report. Sometimes, they may omit information that readers deem important.

Omitted details can cause problems during research evaluation. For instance, it is common for researchers to describe in general terms the questionnaires and attitude scales they used without reporting the exact wording of the questions.[11] Yet there is considerable research indicating that how items are worded can affect the results of a study.

As students apply the evaluation questions in the remaining chapters of this book while evaluating research, they may often find that they must answer "insufficient information to make a judgment."

✓ Guideline 9: Some published research is obviously flawed.

Comment: With many hundreds of editors of and contributors to academic journals, it is understandable that published research reports vary in quality, with some being very obviously weak in terms of their research methodology.[12]

Undoubtedly, some weak reports simply slip past less-skilled editors. More likely, an editor may make a deliberate decision to publish a weak report because the problem it explores is of current interest to the journal's readers. This is especially true when there is a new topic of interest, such as a new educational reform, a newly recognized disease, or a new government initiative. The editorial board of a journal might reasonably conclude that publishing studies on such new topics is important, even if the initial studies are weak.

---

[11] This statement appears in each issue of *The Gallup Poll Monthly*: "In addition to sampling error, readers should bear in mind that question wording…can introduce additional systematic error or 'bias' into the results of opinion polls." Accordingly, *The Gallup Poll Monthly* reports the exact wording of the questions it uses in its polls. Other researchers cannot always do this because the measures they use may be too long to include in the report or may be copyrighted by publishers who do not want the items released to the public.

[12] Many journals are refereed. This means that the editor has experts who act as referees by evaluating each paper submitted for possible publication. These experts make their judgments without knowing the identification of the researcher who submitted the paper, and the editor uses their input in deciding which papers to publish as journal articles.

Sometimes, studies with very serious methodological problems are labeled as *pilot studies*, in either their titles or introductions to the research reports. A pilot study is a preliminary study that allows a researcher to try out new methods and procedures for conducting research, often with small samples. Pilot studies may be refined in subsequent, more definitive studies. Publication of pilot studies, despite their limited samples and other potential weaknesses, is justified on the basis that they may point other researchers in the direction of promising new leads and methods for further research.

✓ Guideline 10: No research report provides "proof."

Comment: Conducting research is fraught with pitfalls, any one study may have very misleading results, and all studies can be presumed to be flawed to some extent. In light of this, individual research reports should be evaluated carefully to identify those that are most likely to provide sound results. In addition, a consumer of research should consider the entire body of research on a given problem. If different researchers using different research methods with different types of strengths and weaknesses all reach similar conclusions, consumers of research may say that they have *considerable confidence* in the conclusions of the body of research. On the other hand, to the extent that the body of research on a topic yields mixed results, consumers of research should lower their degree of confidence. For instance, if all the studies judged to be strong point in one direction while weaker ones point in a different direction, consumers of research might say that they have *some confidence* in the conclusion suggested by the stronger studies.

✓ Guideline 11: Other things being equal, research related to theories is more important than nontheoretical research.

Comment: A given theory helps explain interrelationships among a number of variables and often has implications for understanding human behavior in a variety of settings. Studies that have results consistent with a theory lend support to the theory. Those with inconsistent results argue against the theory. After a number of studies relating to the theory have been conducted, their results provide accumulated evidence that argues for or against the theory and evidence that can assist in modifying the theory. Often, researchers explicitly discuss theories that are relevant to their research, as illustrated in Example 1.11.1.

Example 1.11.1[13]
Portions of researchers' discussion of a theory related to their research:
One of the most influential theories regarding women's intentions to stay in or leave abusive relationships is social exchange theory, which suggests that these kinds of relational decisions follow from an analysis of the relative cost-benefit

[13] Gordon, K. C., Burton, S., & Porter, L. (2004). Predicting the intentions of women in domestic violence shelters to return to partners: Does forgiveness play a role? *Journal of Family Psychology, 18*, 331–338.

ratio of remaining in a relationship (Kelley & Thibaut, 1978). On the basis of this theory, many researchers have posited that whereas escaping the abuse may appear to be a clear benefit, the costs associated with leaving the relationship may create insurmountable barriers for many abused women.

The role of theoretical considerations in the evaluation of research is discussed in greater detail in Chapter 4.

✓ Guideline 12: Many researchers acknowledge obvious flaws in their research.

Comment: Many researchers very briefly point out the most obvious flaws in their research. They typically do this in the last section of their reports, which is the Discussion section. While they tend to be brief and deal with only the most obvious problems, these acknowledgments can be a good starting point in the evaluation of a research report.

Example 1.12.1 shows the researchers' description of the limitations of their research on Mexican American men's college persistence intentions.

Example 1.12.1[14]

Researchers' description of the limitations of their research:

Despite the contributions of this study in expanding our understanding of Mexican American men's college persistence intentions, there also are some clear limitations that should be noted. First, several factors limit our ability to generalize this study's findings to other populations of Mexican American male undergraduates. The participants attended a Hispanic-serving 4-year university in a predominantly Mexican American midsize southern Texas town located near the U.S.-México border. While the majority of U.S. Latinos live in the Southwest region, Latinos are represented in communities across the U.S. (U.S. Census Bureau, 2008c). Additionally, the study's generalizability is limited by the use of nonrandom sampling methods (e.g., self-selection bias) and its cross-sectional approach (Heppner, Wampold, & Kivlighan, 2007).

✓ Guideline 13: To become an expert on a topic, one must become an expert at evaluating original reports of research.

Comment: An expert is someone who knows not only broad generalizations about a topic but also the nuances of the research that underlie them. In other words, he or she knows the particular strengths and weaknesses of the major studies used to arrive at the generalizations. Put another way, an expert on a topic knows the *quality of the evi-*

---

[14] Ojeda, L., Navarro, R. L., & Morales, A. (2011). The role of *la familia* on Mexican American men's college persistence intentions. *Psychology of Men & Masculinity*, *12*, 216–229.

dence regarding that topic and bases generalizations from the research literature on that knowledge.

Exercise for Chapter 1

Part A

Directions: The 13 guidelines discussed in this chapter are repeated below. For each one, indicate the extent to which you were already familiar with it before reading this chapter. Use a scale from 5 (very familiar) to 1 (not at all familiar).

Guideline 1: Researchers often examine narrowly defined problems.

Familiarity rating: 5 4 3 2 1

Guideline 2: Researchers often conduct studies in artificial settings.

Familiarity rating: 5 4 3 2 1

Guideline 3: Researchers use less-than-perfect methods of observation.

Familiarity rating: 5 4 3 2 1

Guideline 4: Researchers use less-than-perfect samples.

Familiarity rating: 5 4 3 2 1

Guideline 5: Even a straightforward analysis of data can produce misleading results.

Familiarity rating: 5 4 3 2 1

Guideline 6: Even a single, isolated flaw in research methods can lead to seriously misleading results.

Familiarity rating: 5 4 3 2 1

Guideline 7: Research reports often contain many details, which can be very important when evaluating a report.

Familiarity rating: 5 4 3 2 1

Guideline 8: Many reports lack information on matters that are potentially important for evaluating a research article.

Familiarity rating: 5 4 3 2 1

Guideline 9: Some published research is obviously flawed.

Familiarity rating: 5 4 3 2 1

Guideline 10: No research report provides "proof."

Familiarity rating: 5 4 3 2 1

Guideline 11: Other things being equal, research related to theories is more important than nontheoretical research.

Familiarity rating: 5 4 3 2 1

Guideline 12: Many researchers acknowledge obvious flaws in their research.

Familiarity rating: 5 4 3 2 1

Guideline 13: To become an expert on a topic, one must become an expert at evaluating original reports of research.

Familiarity rating: 5 4 3 2 1

Part B: Application

Directions: Read a report of research published in an academic journal, and respond to the following questions. The report may be one that you select or one that is assigned by your instructor. If you are using this book without any prior training in research methods, do the best you can in answering the questions at this point. As you work through this book, your evaluations will become increasingly sophisticated.

1. How narrowly is the research problem defined? In your opinion, is it too narrow? Is it too broad? Explain.

2. Was the research setting artificial (e.g., a laboratory setting)? If yes, do you think that the gain in the control of extraneous variables offsets the potential loss of information that would be obtained in a study in a more real-life setting? Explain.

3. Are there any obvious flaws or weaknesses in the researcher's methods of observation? Explain. (Note: Observation is usually described under the subheading Measures.)

4. Are there any obvious sampling flaws? Explain.

5. Was the analysis statistical *or* nonstatistical? Was the description of the results easy to understand? Explain.

6. Were the descriptions of procedures and methods of observation sufficiently detailed? Were any important details missing? Explain.

7. Does the report lack information on matters that are potentially important for evaluating it?

8. Overall, was the research obviously very weak? If yes, briefly describe its weaknesses and speculate on why it was published despite them.

9. Does the researcher describe related theories?

10. Does the researcher imply that his or her research proves something? Do you believe that it proves something? Explain.

11. Do you think that as a result of reading this chapter and evaluating a research report you are becoming more expert at evaluating research reports? Explain.

Chapter 2

Evaluating Titles

Titles help consumers of research to identify journal articles of interest to them. A preliminary evaluation of a title should be made when it is first encountered. After the article is read, the title should be reevaluated to ensure that it accurately reflects the contents of the article.

Apply the questions that follow while evaluating titles. The questions are stated as "yes–no" questions, where a "yes" indicates that you judge the characteristic to be satisfactory. You may also want to rate each characteristic using a scale from 1 to 5, where 5 is the highest rating. N/A (not applicable) and I/I (insufficient information to make a judgment) may also be used when necessary.

___ 1. Is the title sufficiently specific?

Very satisfactory 5 4 3 2 1 Very unsatisfactory ***or*** N/A I/I

Comment: On any major topic in the social and behavioral sciences, there are likely to be many hundreds of research reports published in academic journals. In order to help potential readers locate those that are most relevant to their needs, researchers should use titles that are sufficiently specific so that each article can be differentiated from the other research articles on the same topic.

Consider the topic of depression, which has been extensively investigated. The title in Example 2.1.1 is insufficiently specific. Contrast it with the titles in Example 2.1.2, each of which contains information that differentiates it from the others.

Example 2.1.1

A title that is insufficiently specific:

An Investigation of Adolescent Depression and Its Implications

Example 2.1.2

Three titles that are more specific than the one in Example 2.1.1:

Gender Differences in the Expression of Depression by Early Adolescent Children of Alcoholics

The Impact of Social Support on the Severity of Postpartum Depression Among Adolescent Mothers

The Effectiveness of Cognitive Therapy in the Treatment of Adolescent Students With Severe Clinical Depression

___ 2. Is the title reasonably concise?

Very satisfactory 5 4 3 2 1 Very unsatisfactory ***or*** N/A I/I

Comment: While a title should be specific (see the previous evaluation question), it should be fairly concise. Titles of research articles in academic journals typically are 15 words or less. When a title contains more than 20 words, it is likely that the researcher is providing more information than is needed by consumers of research who want to locate articles.[1]

___ 3. Are the primary variables referred to in the title?

Very satisfactory 5 4 3 2 1 Very unsatisfactory ***or*** N/A I/I

Comment: Variables are the characteristics that vary from one participant to another. In Example 2.3.1, the variables are (1) television viewing habits, (2) mathematics achievement, and (3) reading achievement. For instance, the children *vary* (or differ) in their reading achievement, with some children achieving more than others. Likewise, they vary in terms of their mathematics achievement and their television viewing habits.

Example 2.3.1
A title that mentions three variables:
The Relationship Between Young Children's Television Viewing Habits and Their Achievement in Mathematics and Reading

Note that "young children" is *not* a variable because the title clearly suggests that only young children were studied. In other words, being a young child does not vary in this study. Instead, it is a *common trait* of all the participants.

___ 4. When there are many variables, are the *types* of variables referred to?

Very satisfactory 5 4 3 2 1 Very unsatisfactory ***or*** N/A I/I

Comment: When researchers examine many specific variables in a given study, they may refer to the *types* of variables in their titles rather than naming each one individually. For instance, suppose a researcher administered a standardized achievement test that measured spelling ability, reading comprehension, vocabulary knowledge, mathematical problem-solving skills, and so on. Naming all these variables would create a title that is too long. Instead, the researcher could refer to this collection of variables measured by the test as *academic achievement*, which is done in Example 2.4.1.

[1] Titles of theses and dissertations tend to be longer than those of journal articles.

Example 2.4.1

A title in which types of variables (achievement variables) are identified without being named specifically:

The Relationship Between Parental Involvement in Schooling and Academic Achievement in the Middle Grades

___ **5. Does the title identify the types of individuals who participated?**

Very satisfactory 5 4 3 2 1 Very unsatisfactory ***or*** N/A I/I

Comment: It is often desirable to include names of populations in the title. From the title in Example 2.5.1, it is reasonable to infer that the population of interest consists of graduate students who are taking a statistics class. This would be of interest to a consumer of research who is searching through a list of the many hundreds of published articles on cooperative learning. For instance, knowing that the report deals with this particular population might help a consumer rule it out as an article of interest if he or she is trying to locate research on cooperative learning in elementary school mathematics.

Example 2.5.1

A title in which the type of participants is mentioned:

Effects of Cooperative Learning in a Graduate-Level Statistics Class

Example 2.5.2 also names an important characteristic of the research participants—the fact that they are registered nurses employed by public hospitals.

Example 2.5.2

A title in which the type of participants is mentioned:

Administrative Management Styles and Job Satisfaction Among Registered Nurses Employed by Public Hospitals

Often, researchers use a particular group of participants only because they are readily available, such as college students enrolled in an introductory psychology class who are required to participate in research projects. Researchers might use such individuals even though they are conducting research that might apply to all types of individuals. For instance, a researcher might conduct research to test a social relations theory that might apply to all types of individuals. In such a case, the researcher might omit mentioning the types of individuals (e.g., college students) in the title because the research is not specifically directed at that population.

___ 6. If a study is strongly tied to a theory, is the name of the specific theory mentioned in the title?

Very satisfactory 5 4 3 2 1 Very unsatisfactory ***or*** N/A I/I

Comment: Theories help to advance science because they are propositions regarding relationships that have applications in many diverse, specific situations. For instance, a particular learning theory might have applications for teaching kindergarten children as well as for training astronauts. A useful theory leads to predictions about human behavior that can be tested through research. Many consumers of research are seeking information on specific theories, and mention of them in titles helps these consumers to identify reports of relevant research. Thus, when research is closely tied to a theory, the theory should be mentioned. Example 2.6.1 shows two titles in which specific theories are mentioned.

Example 2.6.1
Two titles that mention specific theories (desirable):

Application of Terror Management Theory to Treatment of Rural Battered Women

Achievement in Science-Oriented Charter Schools for Girls: A Critical Test of the Social Learning Theory

Note that simply using the term *theory* in a title without mentioning the name of the specific theory is not useful to consumers of research. Example 2.6.2 has this undesirable characteristic.

Example 2.6.2
A title that refers to theory without naming the specific theory (undesirable):

An Examination of Voting Patterns and Social Class in a Rural Southern Community: A Study Based on Theory

___ 7. Has the author avoided describing results in the title?

Very satisfactory 5 4 3 2 1 Very unsatisfactory ***or*** N/A I/I

Comment: It is usually inappropriate for a title to describe the results of a research project. Research often raises more questions than it answers. In addition, the results of research are often subject to more than one interpretation. Given that titles need to be concise, attempting to state results in a title is likely to lead to oversimplification.

Consider the title in Example 2.7.1, which undoubtedly oversimplifies the results of the study. A meaningful accounting of the results should address issues such as the following: What type of social support (e.g., parental support, peer support, and so on) is effective? How strong does it need to be to lessen the depression? By how much is depression lessened by strong social support? Because it is almost always impossible to state results accurately and unambiguously in a short title, results ordinarily should *not* be stated at all, as illustrated in the Improved Version of Example 2.7.1.

Example 2.7.1
A title that inappropriately describes results:
Strong Social Support Lessens Depression in Delinquent Young Adolescents

Improved Version of Example 2.7.1
A title that appropriately does not describe results:
The Relationship Between Social Support and Depression in Delinquent Young Adolescents

___ 8. Has the author avoided using a "yes–no" question as a title?

Very satisfactory 5 4 3 2 1 Very unsatisfactory ***or*** N/A I/I

Comment: Because research rarely yields simple, definitive answers, it is seldom appropriate to use a title that poses a simple "yes–no" question. For instance, the title in Example 2.8.1 implies that there is a simple answer to the question it poses. However, a study on this topic undoubtedly explores *the extent to which men and women differ in their opinions on social justice issues*—a much more interesting topic than suggested by the title. The Improved Version is cast as a statement and is more appropriate as the title of a research report for publication in an academic journal.

Example 2.8.1
A title that inappropriately poses a "yes–no" question:
Do Men and Women Differ in Their Opinions on Social Justice Issues?

Improved Version of Example 2.8.1
A title as a statement:
Gender Differences in Opinions on Social Justice Issues

___ 9. If there are a main title and a subtitle, do both provide important information about the research?

Very satisfactory 5 4 3 2 1 Very unsatisfactory ***or*** N/A I/I

Comment: Failure on this evaluation question often results from an author's use of a "clever" main title that is vague, followed by a subtitle that identifies the specific content of the research report. Example 2.9.1 illustrates this problem. In this example, the main title fails to impart specific information. In fact, it could apply to many thousands of studies in hundreds of fields, as diverse as psychology and physics, in which researchers find that various combinations of variables (the parts) contribute to our understanding of a complex whole.

Example 2.9.1
A two-part title with a vague main title (inappropriate):

The Whole Is Greater Than the Sum of Its Parts: The Relationship Between Playing With Pets and Longevity Among the Elderly

Example 2.9.2 is also deficient because the main title is vague.

Example 2.9.2
A two-part title with a vague main title (inappropriate):

The Other Side of the Story: The Relationship Between Social Class and Mothers' Involvement in Their Children's Schooling

In contrast to the previous two examples, Example 2.9.3 has a main title and a subtitle that both refer to specific variables examined in a research study. The first part names two major variables ("attachment" and "well-being"), while the second part names the two groups that were compared in terms of these variables.

Example 2.9.3
A two-part title in which both parts provide important information:

Attachment to Parents and Emotional Well-Being: A Comparison of African American and White Adolescents

The title in Example 2.9.3 could be rewritten as a single statement without a subtitle, as illustrated in Example 2.9.4.

Example 2.9.4
A rewritten version of Example 2.9.3:

A Comparison of the Emotional Well-Being and Attachment to Parents of African American and White Adolescents

Examples 2.9.3 and 2.9.4 are equally good. The evaluation question being considered here is neutral on whether a title should be broken into a main title and subtitle. Rather, it suggests that if it is broken into two parts, both parts should provide important information specific to the research being reported.

___ 10. If the title implies causality, does the method of research justify it?

Very satisfactory 5 4 3 2 1 Very unsatisfactory ***or*** N/A I/I

Comment: Example 2.10.1 implies that causal relationships (i.e., cause-and-effect relationships) have been examined because it contains the word *effects*. This is a keyword frequently used by researchers in their titles to indicate that they have explored causality in their studies.

Example 2.10.1
A title in which causality is implied by the word effects:
The Effects of Computer-Assisted Instruction in Mathematics on Students' Computational Skills

A common method for examining causal relationships is conducting an *experiment.* An experiment is a study in which researchers give treatments to participants to determine whether the treatments *cause* changes.

In a traditional experiment, different groups of participants are given different treatments (e.g., one group receives computer-assisted instruction while a more traditional method is used to teach another group). The researcher compares the outcomes obtained through the application of the various treatments.[2] When such a study is conducted, the use of the word *effects* in the title is justified.[3]

The title in Example 2.10.2 also suggests that the researcher examined a causal relationship because of the inclusion of the word *effects*. Note that in this case, however, the researcher probably did *not* investigate the relationship using an experiment because it would be unethical to manipulate breakfast as an independent variable (i.e., researchers would not want to assign some students to receive breakfast while denying it to others for the purposes of an experiment).

Example 2.10.2
A title in which causality is implied by the word effects:
The Effects of Breakfast on Student Achievement in the Primary Grades

When it is not possible to conduct an experiment on a causal issue, researchers often conduct what are called *ex post facto studies* (also called *causal-comparative studies*). In these studies, researchers identify students who differ on some outcome (such as students who are high and low in achievement in the primary grades) but who are the same on demographics and other potentially influential variables (such as parents' highest level of education, parental income, quality of the schools the children attend, and so on). Comparing the breakfast-eating habits of the two groups (i.e., high- and low-achievement groups) might yield some useful information on whether eating breakfast *affects*[4] students' achievement because the two groups are similar on other variables that might account for differences in achievement (e.g., their parents' level of education is similar). If a researcher has conducted such a study, the use of the word *effects* in the title is justified.

---

[2] Experiments can also be conducted by treating a given person or group differently *at different points in time.* For instance, a researcher might praise a child for staying in his or her seat in the classroom on some days and not praise him or her on others and then compare the child's seat-staying behavior under the two conditions.
[3] The evaluation of experiments is considered in Chapter 9. Note that this evaluation question merely asks if there is a basis for suggesting causality in the title. This evaluation question does not ask for an evaluation of the quality of the experiment or ex post facto study.
[4] Note that in reference to an outcome caused by some treatment, the word is spelled *effects* (i.e., it is a noun). As a verb meaning "to influence," the word is spelled *affects.*

Note that simply examining a relationship without controlling for potentially confounding variables does *not* justify a reference to causality in the title. For instance, if a researcher merely compared the achievement of children who regularly eat breakfast with those who do not without controlling for other explanatory variables, a causal conclusion (and, hence, a title suggesting it) usually cannot be justified.

Also note that synonyms for *effect* are *influence* and *impact*. They should usually be reserved for use in titles of studies that are either experiments or ex post facto studies.

___ 11. Is the title free of jargon and acronyms that might be unknown to the audience for the research report?

Very satisfactory 5 4 3 2 1 Very unsatisfactory ***or*** N/A I/I

Comment: Professionals in all fields use jargon and acronyms (i.e., shorthand for words, usually in capital letters) for efficient and accurate communication with their peers. However, their use in titles of research reports is inappropriate unless the researchers are writing exclusively for such peers. Consider Example 2.11.1. If ACOA is likely to be well-known to all the readers of the journal in which this title appears, its use is probably appropriate. Otherwise, it should be spelled out or have its meaning paraphrased. As you can see, it can be difficult to make this judgment without being familiar with the journal and its audience.[5]

Example 2.11.1

A title with an acronym that is not spelled out (may be inappropriate if not well–known by the reading audience):

Job Satisfaction and Motivation to Succeed Among ACOA in Managerial Positions

___ 12. Are any highly unique or very important characteristics of the study referred to in the title?

Very satisfactory 5 4 3 2 1 Very unsatisfactory ***or*** N/A I/I

Comment: On many topics in the social and behavioral sciences, there may be hundreds of studies. To help readers identify those with highly unusual or very important characteristics, reference to them should be made in the title. For instance, in Example 2.12.1, the mention of a "nationally representative sample" may help distinguish that study from many others employing only local convenience samples.

[5] ACOA stands for Adult Children of Alcoholics.

Example 2.12.1

A title that points out an important strength in sampling:

The Relationship Between Teachers' Job Satisfaction and Compensation in a Nationally Representative Sample

___ **13. Overall, is the title effective and appropriate?**

Very satisfactory 5 4 3 2 1 Very unsatisfactory ***or*** N/A I/I

Comment: Rate this evaluation question after considering your answers to the earlier ones in this chapter, and taking into account any additional considerations and concerns you may have after reading the entire research article.

Exercise for Chapter 2

Part A

Directions: Evaluate each of the following titles to the extent that it is possible to do so without reading the complete research reports. The references for the titles are given below. All are from journals that are widely available in large academic libraries. More definitive application of the evaluation criteria for titles is made possible by reading the articles in their entirety and then evaluating their titles. Keep in mind that there can be considerable subjectivity in determining whether a title is adequate.

1. Does Cultural Capital Really Affect Academic Achievement? New Evidence From Combined Sibling and Panel Data[6]

2. Being a Sibling[7]

3. Estimating the Potential Health Impact and Costs of Implementing a Local Policy for Food Procurement to Reduce the Consumption of Sodium in the County of Los Angeles[8]

4. More Than Numbers Matter: The Effect of Social Factors on Behaviour and Welfare of Laboratory Rodents and Non-Human Primates[9]

5. Social Support Provides Motivation and Ability to Participate in Occupation[10]

---

[6] Jaeger, M. M. (2011). *Sociology of Education, 84*, 281.
[7] Baumann, S. L., Dyches, T. T., & Braddick, M. (2005). *Nursing Science Quarterly, 18*, 51.
[8] Gase, L. N., Kuo, T., Dunet, D., Schmidt, S. M., Simon, P. A., & Fielding, J. E. (2011). *American Journal of Public Health, 101*, 1501.
[9] Olsson, I. A. S., & Westlund, K. (2007). *Applied Animal Behaviour Science, 103*, 229.
[10] Isaksson, G., Lexell, J., & Skär, L. (2007). *OTJR: Occupation, Participation and Health, 27*, 23.

6. Cognitive Abilities of Musicians[11]

7. Social Exclusion Decreases Prosocial Behavior[12]

8. ICTs, Social Thinking and Subjective Well-Being: The Internet and Its Representations in Everyday Life[13]

9. Child Care and Mothers' Mental Health: Is High-Quality Care Associated With Fewer Depressive Symptoms?[14]

10. Education: Theory, Practice, and the Road Less Followed[15]

11. Wake Me Up When There's a Crisis: Progress on State Pandemic Influenza Ethics Preparedness[16]

12. Teachers' Perceptions of Integrating Information and Communication Technologies Into Literacy Instruction: A National Survey in the United States[17]

13. Provincial Laws on the Protection of Women in China: A Partial Test of Black's Theory[18]

Part B

Directions: Examine several academic journals that publish on topics of interest to you. Identify two with titles you think are especially strong in terms of the evaluation questions presented in this chapter. Also, identify two titles that you believe have clear weaknesses. Bring the four titles to class for discussion.

---

[11] Giovagnoli, A. R., & Raglio, A. (2011). *Perceptual and Motor Skills*, *113*, 563.
[12] Twenge, J. M., Baumeister, R. F., DeWall, C. N., Ciarocco, N. J., & Bartels, J. M. (2007). *Journal of Personality and Social Psychology*, *92*, 56.
[13] Contarello, A., & Sarrica, M. (2007). *Computers in Human Behavior*, *23*, 1016.
[14] Gordon, R., Usdansky, M. L., Wang, X., & Gluzman, A. (2011). *Family Relations*, *60*, 446.
[15] Klaczynski, P. A. (2007). *Journal of Applied Developmental Psychology*, *28*, 80.
[16] Thomas, J. C., & Young, S. (2011). *American Journal of Public Health*, *101*, 2080.
[17] Hutchison, A., & Reinking, D. (2011). *Reading Research Quarterly*, *46*, 312.
[18] Lu, H., & Miethe, T. D. (2007). *International Journal of Offender Therapy and Comparative Criminology*, *51*, 25.

Chapter 3

Evaluating Abstracts

An abstract is a summary of a research report that appears below its title. Like the title, it helps consumers of research identify articles of interest. This function of abstracts is so important that the major computerized databases in the social and behavioral sciences provide the abstracts as well as the titles of the articles they index.

Many journals have a policy on the maximum length of abstracts. It is common to allow a maximum of 100 to 250 words.[1] When evaluating abstracts, you will need to make subjective decisions about how much weight to give to the various elements included within them, given that their length typically is severely restricted.

Make a preliminary evaluation of an abstract when you first encounter it. After reading the associated article, reevaluate the abstract. The evaluation questions that follow are stated as "yes–no" questions, where a "yes" indicates that you judge the characteristic being considered as satisfactory. You may also want to rate each characteristic using a scale from 1 to 5, where 5 is the highest rating. N/A (not applicable) and I/I (insufficient information to make a judgment) may also be used when necessary.

___ 1. Is the purpose of the study referred to or at least clearly implied?

Very satisfactory 5 4 3 2 1 Very unsatisfactory ***or*** N/A I/I

Comment: Many writers begin their abstracts with a brief statement of the purpose of their research. Examples 3.1.1 and 3.1.2 show the first sentences of abstracts in which this was done. Note that even though the word *purpose* is not used in Example 3.1.2, the purpose (i.e., to examine the effects of social support on mental health in a particular population) is clearly implied.

Example 3.1.1[2]

First sentence of an abstract that specifically states the purpose of the study (acceptable):

The purpose of the current investigation is to examine the characteristics of college students with attention-deficit hyperactivity disorder symptoms who misuse their prescribed psychostimulant medications.

---

[1] The *Publication Manual of the American Psychological Association* suggests that an abstract should not exceed 150 words.

[2] Jardin, B., Looby, A., & Earleywine, M. (2011). Characteristics of college students with attention-deficit hyperactivity disorder symptoms who misuse their medications. *Journal of American College Health, 59*, 373–377.

Example 3.1.2[3]
First sentence of an abstract that implies the purpose of the study (also acceptable):
This is a pioneering study examining the effect of different types of social support on the mental health of the physically disabled in mainland China.

___ **2. Does the abstract mention highlights of the research methodology?**

Very satisfactory 5 4 3 2 1 Very unsatisfactory ***or*** N/A I/I

Comment: Given the shortness of an abstract, researchers usually can provide only limited information on their research methodology. However, even brief highlights can be helpful to consumers of research who are looking for research reports of interest. Consider Example 3.2.1, which is taken from an abstract. The fact that the researchers used qualitative methodology employing interviews with small samples is an important methodological characteristic that might set this study apart from others on the same topic.

Example 3.2.1[4]
Excerpt from an abstract that describes highlights of research methodology (desirable):
Second marriages are known to be more fragile than first marriages. To better understand the factors that contribute to this fragility, this qualitative study compared stepfamilies that stayed together with those that separated by collecting interview data from one adult in each of the former (n = 31) and latter (n = 26) stepfamilies.

Likewise, Example 3.2.2 provides important information about research methodology (the fact that a telephone survey was used).

Example 3.2.2[5]
Excerpt from an abstract that describes highlights of research methodology (desirable):
Data were collected via telephone survey with the use of a 42-item survey instrument.

[3] Wu, Q., & Mok, B. (2007). Mental health and social support: A pioneering study on the physically disabled in Southern China. *International Journal of Social Welfare*, *16*, 41–54.
[4] Saint-Jacques, M.-C., Robitaille, C., Godbout, É., Parent, C., Drapeau, S., & Gagne, M.-H. (2011). The process distinguishing stable from unstable stepfamily couples: A qualitative analysis. *Family Relations*, *60*, 545–561.
[5] Miller, L. M. (2011). Emergency contraceptive pill (ECP) use and experiences at college health centers in the mid-Atlantic United States: Changes since ECP went over-the-counter. *Journal of American College Health*, *59*, 683–689.

___ 3. Has the researcher omitted the titles of measures (except when these are the focus of the research)?

Very satisfactory 5 4 3 2 1 Very unsatisfactory ***or*** N/A I/I

Comment: Including the full, formal titles of published measures such as tests, questionnaires, and scales in an abstract is *usually* inappropriate (see the exception below) because their names take up space that could be used to convey more important information. Note that consumers of research who are interested in the topic will be able to find the full names of the measures in the body of the research report, where space is less limited than in an abstract. A comparison of Example 3.3.1 and Example 3.3.2 shows how much space can be saved by omitting the names of the measures while conveying the same essential information.

Example 3.3.1

An excerpt from an abstract that names the titles of measures (inappropriate due to space limitations in abstracts):

A sample of 483 college males completed the Attitudes Toward Alcohol Scale (Fourth Edition, Revised), the Alcohol Use Questionnaire, and the Manns-Herschfield Quantitative Inventory of Alcohol Dependence (Brief Form).

Example 3.3.2

An improved version of Example 3.3.1:

A sample of 483 college males completed measures of their attitudes toward alcohol, their alcohol use, and their dependence on alcohol.

The exception: If the primary purpose of the research is to evaluate the reliability and validity of one or more specific measures, it is appropriate to name them in the abstract as well as in the title. This will help readers who are interested in locating research on the characteristics of specific measures. In Example 3.3.3, mentioning the name of a specific measure is appropriate because the purpose of the research is to determine a characteristic of the measure (its reliability).

Example 3.3.3

Excerpt from an abstract that provides the title of a measure (appropriate because the purpose of the research is to investigate the measure):

Test-retest reliability of the Test of Variables of Attention (T.O.V.A.) was investigated in two studies using two different time intervals: 90 min and 1 week (7 days). To investigate the 90-min reliability, 31 school-age children (M = 10 years, SD = 2.66) were administered the T.O.V.A., then re-administered the test....

___ 4. Are the highlights of the results described?

Very satisfactory 5 4 3 2 1 Very unsatisfactory ***or*** N/A I/I

Comment: Example 3.4.1 shows the last three sentences of an abstract, which describe the highlights of the results of a study. Notice that the researchers make general statements about their results, such as "working-class women, in particular, view marriage less favorably," without stating precisely how much less favorably. General statements of this type are acceptable given the need for brevity in an abstract. In other words, it is acceptable to point out highlights of the results in general terms.

Example 3.4.1[6]
Last three sentences of abstract (highlights of results reported):
More than two thirds of respondents mentioned concerns with divorce. Working-class women, in particular, view marriage less favorably than do their male and middle-class counterparts, in part because they see marriage as hard to exit and are reluctant to assume restrictive gender roles. Middle-class cohabitors are more likely to have concrete wedding plans and believe that marriage signifies a greater commitment than does cohabitation.

Note that there is nothing inherently wrong with providing specific statistical results in an abstract if space permits and the statistics are understandable within the limited context of an abstract. Example 3.4.2 illustrates how this might be done.

Example 3.4.2[7]
Part of an abstract with some specific results reported as highlights:
Sixty-nine percent (69%) of respondents were overweight or obese. Nearly half (48%) of respondents reported a diagnosis of a chronic health condition. The most frequently mentioned barriers to weight loss were current eating habits, time, and current physical condition. The most frequently mentioned motivators for losing weight were health, appearance, and feeling better. Sixty-eight (68%) of respondents were interested in losing weight. Women were more likely than men to have an accurate perception of their weight and a greater interest in losing weight.

___ 5. If the study is strongly tied to a theory, is the theory mentioned in the abstract?

Very satisfactory 5 4 3 2 1 Very unsatisfactory ***or*** N/A I/I

---

[6] Miller, A. J., Sassler, S., & Kusi-Appouh, D. (2011). The specter of divorce: Views from working- and middle-class cohabitors. *Family Relations*, *60*, 602–616.
[7] Webber, K. H., & Quintiliani, L. (2011). Development of a weight loss program for Appalachian Kentucky adults: A formative research survey. *Family & Consumer Sciences Research Journal*, *40*, 74–84.

Comment: As indicated in the previous chapter, a theory that is central to a study might be mentioned in the title. If such a theory is not mentioned in the title, it should be mentioned in the abstract, as illustrated in Example 3.5.1. It is also acceptable to mention it in both the title and abstract, as illustrated in Example 3.5.2. (Note that bold italics have been used in these examples for emphasis.)

Example 3.5.1[8]

Title and abstract in which a specific theory is named in the abstract but not in the title (acceptable to de-emphasize theory):

Title: Self-Efficacy Program to Prevent Osteoporosis Among Chinese Immigrants

Objectives: The aim of this study was to evaluate the preliminary effectiveness of an educational intervention based on the ***self-efficacy theory*** aimed at increasing the knowledge of osteoporosis and adoption of preventive behaviors, including regular exercise and osteoporosis medication adherence, designed for Chinese immigrants, aged 45 years or above, living in the United States.

Example 3.5.2[9]

Title and abstract in which a specific theory is mentioned in the title and abstract (acceptable to emphasize theory):

Title: Understanding Alcohol Consumption and Its Correlates Among African American Youths in Public Housing: A Test of ***Problem Behavior Theory***

Abstract: African American youths are overrepresented in urban public housing developments characterized by violence, poverty, and alternative market activities. Using Jessor and Jessor's ***problem behavior theory (PBT)***, the authors examined alcohol use and its correlates in a sample of African American youths from three public housing developments (N = 403). Multiple logistic regression analyses were performed to estimate the relative contributions of demographics, personality, environment, and behavior system variables in predicting past-year alcohol use. Results provide support for PBT. Depressive effects and causes were significant predictors of adolescent alcohol use. Delinquent behavior and affiliation with delinquent peers were also associated with alcohol use. Furthermore, age was related to alcohol use. Implications for practice and future inquiry are suggested.

---

[8] Qi, B.-B., Resnick, B., Smeltzer, S. C., & Bausell, B. (2011). Self-efficacy program to prevent osteoporosis among Chinese immigrants. *Nursing Research, 60*, 393–404.

[9] Lombe, M., Yu, M., Nebbitt, V., & Earl, T. (2011). Understanding alcohol consumption and its correlates among African American youths in public housing: A test of problem behavior theory. *Social Work Research, 35*, 173–182.

___ 6. Has the researcher avoided making vague references to implications and future research directions?

Very satisfactory 5 4 3 2 1 Very unsatisfactory ***or*** N/A I/I

Comment: Most researchers discuss the implications of their research and directions for future research near the end of their reports. The limited amount of space allotted to abstracts usually should not be used to make vague references to these matters. Example 3.6.1 is the closing sentence from an abstract. It contains vague references to implications and future research.

Example 3.6.1

Last sentence of an abstract with vague references to implications and future research (inappropriate):

This article concludes with a discussion of both the implications of the results and directions for future research.

Example 3.6.1 could safely be omitted from the abstract without causing a loss of important information because most readers will correctly assume that most research reports discuss these elements. An alternative is to state something specific about these matters, as illustrated in Example 3.6.2. Notice that in this example, the researcher does not describe the implications but indicates that the implications will be of special interest to a particular group of professionals—school counselors. This will alert school counselors that this research report (among the many hundreds of others on drug abuse) might be of special interest to them. If space does not permit such a long closing sentence in the abstract, it could be shortened to "Implications for school counselors are discussed."

Example 3.6.2

Improved version of Example 3.6.1 (last sentence of an abstract):

While these results have implications for all professionals who work with adolescents who abuse drugs, special attention is given to the implications for school counselors.

In short, implications and future research do not necessarily need to be mentioned in abstracts. If they are mentioned, however, something specific should be said about them.

___ 7. Overall, is the abstract effective and appropriate?

Very satisfactory 5 4 3 2 1 Very unsatisfactory ***or*** N/A I/I

Comment: Rate this evaluation question after considering your answers to the earlier ones in this chapter, while taking into account any additional considerations and concerns you may have.

When answering this evaluation question, also consider whether all three major elements are included in an abstract. Example 3.7.1 shows the three elements in bold text.

Example 3.7.1[10]
An abstract with the three major elements indicated in bold text (bold headings added for instructional purposes):

Objective: The purpose of this study was to examine challenges and recommendations (identified by college administrators) to enforcing alcohol policies implemented at colleges in the southeastern United States. **Methods**: Telephone interviews were conducted with 71 individuals at 21 institutions. **Results**: Common challenges included inconsistent enforcement, mixed messages received by students, and students' attitudes toward alcohol use. The most common recommendations were ensuring a comprehensive approach, collaboration with members of the community, and enhanced alcohol education.

Exercise for Chapter 3

Part A

Directions: Evaluate each of the following abstracts (to the extent that it is possible to do so without reading the associated articles) by answering Evaluation Question 7 ("Overall, is the abstract effective and appropriate?") using a scale from 1 (very unsatisfactory) to 5 (very satisfactory). In the explanations for your ratings, refer to the other evaluation questions in this chapter. Point out *both* strengths and weaknesses, if any, of the abstracts.

1. *Title*: Effect of An Aerobic Training Program As Complementary Therapy in Patients With Moderate Depression[11]

   Abstract: The aim of this study was to assess the effects of an aerobic training program as complementary therapy in patients suffering from moderate depression. Eighty-two female patients were divided into a group that received traditional pharmacotherapy (Fluoxetine 20 mg) and a group that received pharmacotherapy plus an aerobic training program. This program was carried out for eight consecutive weeks, three days per week, and included gymnastics, dancing, and walking. Depressive symptoms were measured with the Beck Depression Inventory and the ICD-10 Guide for Depression Diagnosis, both administered before and after treatments. The results confirm the effectiveness of the aerobic training

[10] Cremeens, J. L., Usdan, S. L., Umstattd, M. R., Talbott, L. L., Turner, L., & Perko, M. (2011). Challenges and recommendations to enforcement of alcohol policies on college campuses: An administrator's perspective. *Journal of American College Health, 59*, 427–430.

[11] de la Cerda, P., Cervelló, E., Cocca, A., & Viciana, J. (2011). Effect of an aerobic training program as complementary therapy in patients with moderate depression. *Perceptual and Motor Skills, 112*, 761–769.

program as a complementary therapy to diminish depressive symptoms in patients suffering from moderate depression.

Overall, is the abstract effective and appropriate?

5 4 3 2 1

Explain your rating:

2. *Title*: What's the Problem? A Look at Men in Marital Therapy[12]

Abstract: This study examined the premise that men's lack of awareness of relational problems contributes to their reluctance to consider, seek, and benefit from couples therapy. Ninety-two couples reported on couple and family problem areas using the Dyadic Adjustment Scale and the Family Assessment Device. No gender differences were found in either the frequency or the pattern of initial problem reports or improvement rates during ten sessions of couples therapy at a university training outpatient clinic. Implications for treatment and recommendations for future research are discussed.

Overall, is the abstract effective and appropriate?

5 4 3 2 1

Explain your rating:

3. *Title*: Middle School Drinking: Who, Where, and When [13]

Abstract: The goal of this research was to describe the most common drinking situations for young adolescents (N = 1171; 46.6% girls), as well as determine predictors of their drinking in the seventh and eighth grades. Middle school students most frequently drank at parties with three to four teens, in their home or at a friend's home, and reported alcohol-related problems including conflicts with friends or parents, memory loss, nausea, and doing things they would not normally do. Differences emerged in predicting higher levels of drinking on the basis of sex, race, grade, positive alcohol expectancies, impulsivity, and peer drinking. These findings suggest both specific and general factors are implicated in drinking for middle school students. Contextual factors, including drinking alone, in public places, and at or near school, are characteristic of the most problematic alcohol involvement in middle school and may have utility in prevention and early intervention.

Overall, is the abstract effective and appropriate?

5 4 3 2 1

Explain your rating:

---

[12] Moynehan, J., & Adams, J. (2007). What's the problem? A look at men in marital therapy. *American Journal of Family Therapy*, *3*, 41–51.

[13] Anderson, K. G., & Brown, S. A. (2011). Middle school drinking: Who, where, and when. *Journal of Child & Adolescent Substance Abuse*, *20*, 48–62.

4. *Title*: Adult Attachment Variables Predict Depression Before and After Treatment for Chronic Pain[14]

   Abstract: The complex relationship between chronic pain and depression has long been of clinical and empirical interest. Although attachment theory has been described as a "theory of affect regulation," and has been lauded as a developmental framework for chronic pain, surprisingly little research specifically considers the links between adult attachment variables and pain-related depression. A sample of 99 participants with chronic pain of non-cancer origin was evaluated before and after pain rehabilitation. Results demonstrated that two attachment dimensions (comfort with closeness and relationship anxiety) were related to pre- and posttreatment depression. Of particular interest was the finding that comfort with closeness was the unique predictor of lower levels of posttreatment depression, usurping pain intensity and pretreatment depression. These results are discussed in terms of clinical implications, and suggest that adult attachment theory may prove a valuable perspective in pain treatment programs.

   Overall, is the abstract effective and appropriate?

   5 4 3 2 1

   Explain your rating:

5. *Title*: The Roles of Instructional Practices and Motivation in Writing Performance[15]

   Abstract: The authors investigated what and how instructional practices are related to students' motivation and performance in writing. The participants were 6 teacher interns and their (*N* = 209) secondary-school students in Hong Kong. In a 3-session instruction unit, the teacher interns taught their students how to write an expository essay. The students completed the essay and then a questionnaire to report their motivation in the task and their perception of the instruction. Results of structural equation modeling showed that students' motivation mediated the effects of instructional practices on writing performance. The authors found that when the teachers adopted more motivating teaching strategies, the students were more motivated. When the students were more motivated, they, in turn, had better performance in writing.

   Overall, is the abstract effective and appropriate?

   5 4 3 2 1

   Explain your rating:

---

[14] Meredith, P. J., Strong, J., & Feeney, J. A. (2007). Adult attachment variables predict depression before and after treatment for chronic pain. *European Journal of Pain, 11*, 164–170.

[15] Lam, S.-F., & Law, Y.-K. (2007). The roles of instructional practices and motivation in writing performance. *Journal of Experimental Education, 75*, 145–164.

Part B

Directions: Examine several academic journals that publish on topics of interest to you. Identify two with abstracts that you think are especially strong in terms of the evaluation questions presented in this chapter. Also, identify two abstracts that you believe have clear weaknesses. Bring the four abstracts to class for discussion.

Chapter 4

Evaluating Introductions and Literature Reviews

Research reports in academic journals usually begin with an introduction in which literature is cited.[1] An introduction with an integrated literature review has the following five purposes: (a) introduce the problem area, (b) establish its importance, (c) provide an overview of the relevant literature, (d) show how the current study will advance knowledge in the area, and (e) describe the researcher's specific research questions, purposes, or hypotheses, which usually are stated in the last paragraph of the introduction.

This chapter presents evaluation questions regarding the introductory material in a research report. In the next chapter, the evaluation of the literature review portion is considered.

___ 1. Does the researcher begin by identifying a specific problem area?

Very satisfactory 5 4 3 2 1 Very unsatisfactory ***or*** N/A I/I

Comment: Some researchers start their introductions with statements that are so broad they fail to identify the specific area of investigation. As the beginning of an introduction to a study on the effects of a tobacco control program for military troops, Example 4.1.1 is deficient. Notice that it fails to identify the specific area (tobacco control) to be explored in the research.

Example 4.1.1

Beginning of an inappropriately broad introduction:

The federal government expends considerable resources for research on public health issues, especially as they relate to individuals serving in the military. The findings of this research are used to formulate policies that regulate health-related activities in military settings. In addition to helping establish regulations, agencies develop educational programs so that individuals have appropriate information when making individual lifestyle decisions that may affect their health.

Example 4.1.2 illustrates a more appropriate beginning for a research report on a tobacco control program for the military.

---

[1] In theses and dissertations, the first chapter usually is the introduction, with relatively few references to the literature. This is followed by a chapter that provides a comprehensive literature review.

Example 4.1.2[2]

A specific beginning (compare with Example 4.1.1):

Given the negative health consequences associated with tobacco use and their impact on physical fitness and readiness, the Department of Defense (DoD) has identified the reduction of tobacco use as a priority for improving the health of U.S. military forces (Department of Defense, 1977, 1986, 1994a, 1994b, 1999). Under these directives, tobacco use in official buildings and vehicles is prohibited; information regarding the health consequences of tobacco use is provided at entry into the military; and health care providers are encouraged to inquire about their patients' tobacco use. Recently, the DoD (1999) developed the *Tobacco Use Prevention Strategic Plan* that established DoD-wide goals. These goals include promoting a tobacco-free lifestyle and culture in the military, reducing the rates of cigarette and smokeless tobacco use, decreasing the availability of tobacco products, and providing targeted interventions to identified tobacco users.

Despite DoD directives and programs that focus on tobacco use reduction, the 2002 DoD worldwide survey indicated that past-month cigarette use in all branches of the military increased from 1998 to 2002 (from 29.9% to 33.8%; Bray et al., 2003). This recent increase in military smoking is....

Deciding whether a researcher has started the introduction by being reasonably specific often involves some subjectivity. As a general rule, the researcher should get to the point quickly without using valuable journal space to outline a very broad problem area rather than the specific one(s) that he or she has directly studied.

___ 2. Does the researcher establish the importance of the problem area?

Very satisfactory 5 4 3 2 1 Very unsatisfactory ***or*** N/A I/I

Comment: Researchers select research problems they believe are important, and they should specifically address this belief early in their introductions. Often, this is done by citing previously published statistics that indicate how widespread a problem is, how many individuals are affected by it, and so on. Example 4.2.1 illustrates how researchers did this in the first paragraph of a study on adolescent bulimia.

---

[2] Klesges, R. C., DeBon, M., Vander Weg, M. W., Haddock, C. K., Lando, H. A., Relyea, G. E., ... Talcott, G. W. (2006). Efficacy of a tailored tobacco control program on long-term use in a population of U.S. military troops. *Journal of Consulting and Clinical Psychology*, *74*, 295–306.

Example 4.2.1[3]

First paragraph of an introduction that includes statistics to establish the importance of a problem area:

Bulimic symptoms largely afflict adolescents, typically girls between the ages of 12 and 25 (Lewinsohn, Striegel-Moore, & Seeley, 2000; Woodside & Garfinkel, 1992). For instance, studies of community samples suggest that approximately 2% of girls in junior high and 4% to 9% of girls in high school show clinical levels of bulimic symptoms (Gross & Rosen, 1988; Stein & Brinza, 1989). Furthermore, between 12% and 44% of adolescent girls may exhibit some form of subclinical behaviors (Stice, 2001; Stice, Killen, Hayward, & Taylor, 1998). Because of these alarming statistics, close attention should be paid to potential risk factors and processes associated with the development of bulimic symptoms in adolescence.

Example 4.2.2 also uses statistical information to justify the importance of a study on bullying in school.

Example 4.2.2[4]

Beginning of an introduction that includes statistical information to establish the importance of a problem area:

Peer victimization during school occurs at a rate of 2.4 instances per hour (Atlas, Rona, & Pepler, 1998), with prevalence rates of bullying affecting the lives of more than 30% of all school-age students (Nansel, Overpect, Pilla, Ruan, Simons-Morton, & Scheidt, 2001). Wang, Iannotti, and Nansel (2009) reported that 20.8% of school-age students reported being physically bullied, 53.6% verbally bullied, 51.4% were victims of relational bullying (e.g., repeated insults, circulation of rumors, peer group exclusion), and 13.6% were victims of electronic or cyber-bullying.

Instead of providing statistics on the prevalence of problems, researchers sometimes use other strategies to convince readers of the importance of the research problems they studied. One approach is to show that prominent individuals or influential authors have considered and addressed the issue that is being researched. Another approach is to show that a topic is of current interest because of actions taken by governments (such as legislative actions), major corporations, and professional associations. Example 4.2.3 illustrates the latter technique, in which the actions of both a prominent professional association and state legislatures are cited.

---

[3] Salafia, E. H. B., & Gondoli, D. M. (2011). A 4-year longitudinal investigation of the processes by which parents and peers influence the development of early adolescent girls' bulimic symptoms. *Journal of Early Adolescence*, *31*, 390–414.

[4] Blood, G. W., Blood, I. M., Tramontana, G. M., Sylvia, A. J., Boyle, M. P., & Motzko, G. R. (2011). Self-reported experience of bullying of students who stutter: Relations with life satisfaction, life orientation, and self-esteem. *Perceptual and Motor Skills*, *113*, 353–364.

Example 4.2.3[5]

Beginning of an introduction that uses a nonstatistical argument to establish the importance of a problem:

Less than 10 years after the American Psychological Association (APA) Council officially endorsed prescriptive authority for psychologists and outlined recommended training (APA, 1996), psychologists are prescribing in New Mexico and Louisiana. In both 2005 and again in 2006 seven states and territories introduced prescriptive authority legislation and RxP Task Forces were active in many more states (Sullivan, 2005; Baker, 2006). Commenting on this dramatic maturing of the prescriptive authority agenda, DeLeon (2003, p. XIII) notes it is "fundamentally a social policy agenda ensuring that all Americans have access to the highest possible quality of care...wherein psychotropics are prescribed in the context of an overarching psychologically based treatment paradigm." The agenda for psychologists prescribing is inspired by the premise that psychologists so trained will play central roles in primary health care delivery. Psychologists will then serve at the gateway to the health care system....

Finally, a researcher may attempt to establish the nature and importance of a problem by citing anecdotal evidence or personal experience. While this is arguably the weakest way to establish the importance of a problem, a unique and interesting anecdote might convince readers that the problem is important enough to investigate.

A caveat: When you apply Evaluation Question 2 to the introduction of a research report, do *not* confuse the importance of a problem with your personal interest in the problem. It is possible to have little personal interest in a problem yet still recognize that a researcher has established its importance. On the other hand, it is possible to have a strong personal interest in a problem but judge that the researcher has failed to make a strong argument (or has failed to present convincing evidence) to establish its importance.

___ 3. Are any underlying theories adequately described?

Very satisfactory 5 4 3 2 1 Very unsatisfactory ***or*** N/A I/I

Comment: If a theory is named in the introduction to a research article, the theory should be adequately described. As a general rule, even a well-known theory should be described in at least a short paragraph (along with one or more references where additional information can be found). Lesser-known theories and new theories should be described in more detail.

Example 4.3.1 briefly but clearly summarizes a key aspect of attachment theory, which underlies the authors' research.[6]

---

[5] LeVine, E. S. (2007). Experiences from the frontline: Prescribing in New Mexico. *Psychological Services*, *4*, 59–71.

[6] Only a brief excerpt of the discussion of how the theory might apply is shown in the example.

Example 4.3.1[7]
Excerpt from the introduction to a research article that describes a theory that underlies the research:

Attachment theory can contribute important insights into the long-term impact of early family experiences on the individual's behavior in later relationships. According to that theory, the nature and quality of close relationships in adulthood are strongly influenced by affective events that took place in childhood, particularly within the child-caregiver relationship (Collins & Read, 1990). In the same vein, Bowlby (1977), a leading theorist in the field, argued that the quality of the child-caregiver relationship has a profound impact on the child's developing personality and on the child's concept of self and others. Specifically, children internalize their experiences with caregivers, and those early experiences form a template for later relationships outside the family. Bowlby (1977), referred to those templates as working models, which are carried forward into other relationships and guide the individual's expectations, perceptions, and behavior.

Note that much useful research is *nontheoretical*. Sometimes, the purpose of a study is only to collect and interpret data in order to make a practical decision. For instance, a researcher might poll parents to determine what percentage favors a proposed regulation that would require students to wear uniforms when attending school. Nontheoretical information on parents' attitudes toward requiring uniforms might be an important consideration when a school board is making a decision on the issue.

Another major reason for conducting nontheoretical research is to determine whether there is a problem and/or the incidence of a problem. For instance, without regard to theory, a researcher might collect data on the percentage of pregnant women attending a county medical clinic who use tobacco products during pregnancy. The resulting data will help decision makers determine the prevalence of this problem within the clinic's population.

When applying Evaluation Question 3 to nontheoretical research, "not applicable" (N/A) will usually be the best answer.

A special note for evaluating qualitative research: Often, qualitative researchers explore problem areas without initial reference to theories and hypotheses. Instead, they develop new theories (and models and other generalizations) as they collect and analyze data. The data often take the form of transcripts from open-ended interviews, notes on direct observation and involvement in activities with participants, and so on. Thus, in a research article reporting on qualitative research, a theory might not be described until the Results and Discussion sections (instead of the Introduction). When this is the case, apply Evaluation Question 3 to the point at which theory is discussed.

---

[7] Kulik, L., & Havusha-Morgenstern, H. (2011). Does cohabitation matter? Differences in initial marital adjustment among women who cohabitated and those who did not. *Families in Society: The Journal of Contemporary Social Services*, *92*, 120–127.

___ 4. Does the introduction move from topic to topic instead of from citation to citation?

Very satisfactory 5 4 3 2 1 Very unsatisfactory ***or*** N/A I/I

Comment: Introductions that typically fail on this evaluation question are organized around citations rather than topics. For instance, a researcher might *inappropriately* first summarize Smith's study, then Jones's study, then Doe's study, and so on. The result is a series of annotations that are merely strung together. This fails to show readers how the various sources relate to each other and what they mean as a whole.

In contrast, an introduction should be organized around topics and subtopics, with references cited as needed, often in groups of two or more citations per source. For instance, if four research reports support a certain point, the point usually should be stated with all four references cited together (as opposed to in separate statements or paragraphs that summarize each of the four sources).

In Example 4.4.1, there are three citations for the points made in each of the two sentences.

Example 4.4.1[8]

An excerpt from a literature review with sources cited in groups:

For most individuals facing the end of life, having control over their final days, dying in a place of their choosing, and being treated with dignity and respect are central concerns (Chochinov et al., 2002; Steinhauser et al., 2000; Vig, Davenport, & Pearlman, 2002). However, research suggests that quality end-of-life care is often lacking in [nursing homes], resulting in residents dying with their symptoms poorly managed, their psychological or spiritual needs neglected, and their families feeling dissatisfied with the care provided (Teno, Kabumoto, Wetle, Roy, & Mor, 2004; Thompson, Menec, Chochinov, & McClement, 2008; Wetle, Shield, Teno, Miller, & Welch, 2005).

When a researcher is discussing a particular source that is crucial to a point being made, that source should be discussed in more detail than in Example 4.4.1. However, because research reports in academic journals are expected to be relatively brief, detailed discussions of individual sources should be presented sparingly and only for the most important related literature.

___ 5. Are very long introductions broken into subsections, each with its own subheading?

Very satisfactory 5 4 3 2 1 Very unsatisfactory ***or*** N/A I/I

Comment: When there are a number of issues to be covered in a long introduction, there may be several sub-essays, each with its own subheading. The subheadings help

[8] Thompson, G. N., McClement, S. E., & Chochinov, H. M. (2011). How respect and kindness are experienced at the end of life by nursing home residents. *Canadian Journal of Nursing Research*, *43*, 97–118.

to guide readers through long introductions. For instance, Example 4.5.1 shows the five subheadings used within the introduction to a study of risk and protective factors for alcohol and marijuana use among urban and rural adolescents.

Example 4.5.1[9]

Five subheadings used within an introduction:

Individual Factors

Family Factors

Peer Factors

Community Factors

Risk and Protective Factors Among Urban and Rural Youths

___ 6. Has the researcher provided adequate conceptual definitions of key terms?

Very satisfactory 5 4 3 2 1 Very unsatisfactory ***or*** N/A I/I

Comment: Often, researchers will pause at appropriate points in their introductions to offer formal conceptual definitions,[10] such as the one shown in Example 4.6.1. Note that it is acceptable for a researcher to cite a previously published definition, which is done in the example. Also, note that the researchers contrast the term being defined (i.e., academic self-concept) with a term with which it might be confused (i.e., academic engagement).

Example 4.6.1[11]

A conceptual definition provided in an introduction to a research report:

Academic self-concept refers to perceptions of one's own academic competence, and develops out of past experiences, evaluative feedback from important others, and social comparisons (Dweck, 2002; Harter, 1998). *Academic engagement* refers to enthusiastic and focused involvement in academic activities and manifests in behaviors such as effort and active class participation (Kindermann, 2007; Ryan, 2001). Youths' academic self-concepts and engagement are interrelated: Academic self-concept predicts expectations for success and the value

---

[9] Clark, T. T., Nguyen, A. B., & Belgrave, F. Z. (2011). Risk and protective factors for alcohol and marijuana use among African American rural and urban adolescents. *Journal of Child & Adolescent Substance Abuse*, *20*, 205–220.

[10] A *conceptual definition* identifies a term using only general concepts but with enough specificity that the term is not confused with other related terms or concepts. As such, it resembles a dictionary definition. In contrast, an *operational definition* describes the physical process used to examine a variable. For instance, "psychological control" by parents could be examined with the use of a particular observation checklist, which would be described under the heading Measures later in a research report (see Chapter 8).

[11] Molloy, L. E., Gest, S. D., & Rulison, K. L. (2011). Peer influences on academic motivation: Exploring multiple methods of assessing youths' most "influential" peer relationships. *Journal of Early Adolescence*, *31*, 13–40.

placed on academic achievement, which, in turn, affects levels of academic engagement (e.g., Wigfield & Eccles, 2002).

Conceptual definitions do not need to be lengthy as long as their meaning is clear. The first sentence in Example 4.6.2 shows a brief conceptual definition.

Example 4.6.2[12]
A conceptual definition provided in an introduction to a research report:

In Cobb's (1976) classic disquisition, *social support* is defined as the perception that one is loved, valued and esteemed, and able to count on others should the need arise. The desire and need for social support have evolved as an adaptive tool for survival, and our perceptions of the world around us as being supportive emerge from our interactions and attachments experienced early in the life course (Bowlby, 1969, 1973; Simpson, & Belsky, 2008). Consequent to the seminal review articles of Cobb (1976) and Cassel (1976), a vast and consistent body of evidence has accumulated suggesting that social support from family and friends is protective against a variety of adverse health outcomes.

At times, researchers may not provide formal conceptual definitions because the terms have widespread commonly held definitions. For instance, in a report of research on various methods of teaching handwriting, a researcher may not offer a formal definition of handwriting, which might be acceptable.

In sum, this evaluation question should not be applied mechanically by looking to see if there is a specific statement of a definition. The mere absence of one does not necessarily mean that a researcher has failed on this evaluation question because a conceptual definition is not needed for some variables. When this is the case, you may give the research a rating of N/A ("not applicable") for this evaluation question.

___ 7. Has the researcher cited sources for "factual" statements?

Very satisfactory 5 4 3 2 1 Very unsatisfactory ***or*** N/A I/I

Comment: Researchers should avoid making statements that sound like facts without referring to their source. Example 4.7.1 is deficient in this respect. Compare it with its Improved Version, in which sources are cited for various assertions.

Example 4.7.1
An unreferenced factual claim (undesirable):

Nursing is widely recognized as a high-stress occupation, which is highly demanding, yet has limited resources to support nurses with their occupational stress. Providing palliative care to patients with fatal diseases is especially stressful, causing both emotional and professional challenges for nurses.

---

[12] Gayman, M. D., Turner, R. J., Cislo, A. M., & Eliassen, A. H. (2011). Early adolescent family experiences and perceived social support in young adulthood. *Journal of Early Adolescence*, *31*, 880–908.

Improved Version of Example 4.7.1[13]

Sources cited for factual claims (compare with Example 4.7.1):

Considering the large number of demands and the limited resources available to support them, nurses represent a high-risk group for experiencing occupational stress (Bourbonnais, Comeau, & Vézina, 1999; Demerouti, Bakker, Nachreiner, & Schaufeli, 2000). Numerous studies suggest that those offering palliative care could be particularly at risk (Twycross, 2002; Wilkes et al., 1998). Palliative care provides comfort, support, and quality of life to patients living with fatal diseases, such as cancer (Ferris et al., 2002). Nurses involved in the provision of this type of care meet several recurrent professional, emotional, and organizational challenges (Fillion, Saint-Laurent, & Rousseau, 2003; Lu, While, & Barriball, 2005; Newton & Waters, 2001; Plante & Bouchard, 1995; Vachon, 1995, 1999).

___ 8. Do the specific research purposes, questions, or hypotheses logically flow from the introductory material?

Very satisfactory 5 4 3 2 1 Very unsatisfactory ***or*** N/A I/I

Comment: Typically, the specific research purposes, questions, or hypotheses on which a study is based are stated in the final paragraphs of the introduction.[14] The material preceding them should set the stage and logically lead to them. For instance, if a researcher argues that research methods used by previous researchers are not well suited for answering certain research questions, it would not be surprising to learn that his or her research purpose is to reexamine the research questions using alternative research methods. In Example 4.8.1, which are the last paragraphs in the introduction to a research report, the researchers refer to the literature that they reviewed in the introduction. This sets the stage for the specific research questions, which are stated in the last sentence of the example.

Example 4.8.1[15]

Last paragraphs of an introduction (beginning with a summary of the research that was reviewed and ending with a statement of the purposes of the current research):

Previous research [reviewed above] provides clear support of the importance of teachers' expectations and students' perceptions of teachers' oral feedback. As

[13] Fillion, L., Tremblay, I., Truchon, M., Côté, D., Struthers, C. W., & Dupuis, R. (2007). Job satisfaction and emotional distress among nurses providing palliative care: Empirical evidence for an integrative occupational stress-model. *International Journal of Stress Management, 14*, 1–25.

[14] Some researchers state their research purposes, questions, or hypotheses in general terms near the beginning of their introductions and then restate them more specifically near the end.

[15] Chen, Y.-H., Thompson, M. S., Kromrey, J. D., & Chang, G. H. (2011). Relations of student perceptions of teacher oral feedback with teacher expectancies and student self-concept. *The Journal of Experimental Education, 79*, 452–477.

Babad (1990) noted, "Students' awareness of teachers' differential [behavior] constitutes a critical link in all models explaining teacher expectancy mediation" (p. 683). The present study extends previous research by investigating the tenability of this theory in the context of elementary schools in Taiwan.

We addressed three specific research questions in this study. First, we explored....

___ **9. Overall, is the introduction effective and appropriate?**

Very satisfactory 5 4 3 2 1 Very unsatisfactory ***or*** N/A I/I

Comment: Rate this evaluation question after considering your answers to the earlier ones in this chapter and taking into account any additional considerations and concerns you may have. Be prepared to explain your overall evaluation.

Exercise for Chapter 4

Part A

Directions: Following are the beginning paragraphs of introductions to research articles. Answer the questions that follow each one.

1. Longitudinal and experimental studies on children in orphanages, children's homes, and foster families have confirmed the adverse effects of long-term institutional care on children's personality development (American Academy of Child and Adolescent Psychiatry, 2005; Castle et al., 1999; Chisholm, 1998; Marcovitch et al., 1997; O'Connor, Marvin, Rutter, Olrick, & Britner, 2003; Roy, Rutter, & Pickles, 2000; Tizard & Hodges, 1978; Tizard & Rees, 1975; Vorria, Rutter, Pickles, Wolkind, & Hobsbaum, 1998; Wolkind, 1974; Zeanah, 2000; Zeanah, Smyke, & Dumitrescu, 2002). Consistently reported effects on children's behavior include hyperactivity, inability to concentrate, poor school performance, ineffective coping skills, conduct disorder (CD) symptoms, disruptive attention-seeking, difficulties with peers, few close relationships, emotional withdrawal, and indiscriminate relationships with adults. Similar effects have been observed in adolescents (Hodges & Tizard, 1989a, 1989b), together with an early report of schizoid personality traits (Goldfarb, 1943). Institutional rearing conveys a greater risk of hyperactivity and inattention, compared to foster home rearing (Roy et al., 2000; Vorria et al., 1998).

   Providing subsequent family care and improving the quality of caregivers' parenting skills both reduce the risk of problem behavior (Webster-Stratton, 1998) and improve cognitive development (Loeb, Fuller, Kagan, & Carrol, 2004). These consistent findings have influenced policymakers for child welfare in different countries (Broad, 2001; Department for Education and Skills, 1989; Maunders, 1994; NSW Community Services Commission, 1996) to prioritize foster home or kinships over children's home care and to increase investment to raise standards within care systems.[16]

a. How well have the researchers established the importance of the problem area? Explain.

b. Does the material move from topic to topic instead of from citation to citation? Explain.

c. Have the researchers cited sources for factual statements? Explain.

2. "This man is just not cooperating and just doesn't want to be in therapy." A doctoral student working with a 26-year-old white man in counseling was frustrated at her inability to get her client to reveal what she regarded to be his true feelings. She believed that he was resistant to therapy because of his reticence to show emotions. However, her supervisor, someone trained in the psychology of men, explained to her the difficulty some men have in expressing emotions: that, in fact, some men are unaware of their emotional states. Working with the supervisor, the trainee focused part of the therapy on helping the client identify and normalize his emotions and providing some psychoeducation on the affects of his masculine socialization process. This critical incident could be repeated in psychology training programs around the country. As men come to therapy, the issue for many psychologists becomes How do psychologists become competent to work with men? This question may seem paradoxical given the sentiment that most if not all of psychology is premised on men's, especially white men's, worldviews and experiences (Sue, Arredondo, & McDavis, 1992; Sue & Sue, 2003). But several authors have suggested that working with men in therapy is a clinical competency and just as complex and difficult as working with women and other multicultural communities (Addis & Mahalik, 2003; Liu, 2005).[17]

a. How well have the researchers established the importance of the problem area? Explain.

[16] Yang, M., Ullrich, S., Roberts, A., & Coid, J. (2007). Childhood institutional care and personality disorder traits in adulthood: Findings from the British National Surveys of Psychiatric Morbidity. *American Journal of Orthopsychiatry, 77*, 67–75.

[17] Mellinger, T. N., & Liu, W. M. (2007). Men's issues in doctoral training: A survey of counseling psychology programs. *Professional Psychology: Research and Practice, 37*, 196–204.

Part B

Directions: Following are excerpts from various sections of introductions. Answer the questions that follow each one.

3. The current article focuses on one such intermediate perspective: the dialect theory of communicating emotion. Dialect theory proposes the presence of cultural differences in the use of cues for emotional expression that are subtle enough to allow accurate communication across cultural boundaries in general, yet substantive enough to result in a potential for miscommunication (Elfenbein & Ambady, 2002b, 2003).[18]

   a. Is the theory adequately described? Explain.

4. Terror management theory (see Greenberg et al., 1997, for a complete presentation) is based on the premise that humans are in a precarious position due to the conflict between biological motives to survive and the cognitive capacity to realize life will ultimately end. This generally unconscious awareness that death is inevitable, coupled with proclivities for survival, creates potentially paralyzing anxiety that people manage by investing in a meaningful conception of the world (cultural worldview) that provides prescriptions for valued behavior and thus a way to also maintain self-esteem. For instance, support for the theory has been provided by numerous findings that reminding people of their own eventual death (mortality salience) results in an attitudinal and behavioral defense of their cultural worldview (*worldview defense*, e.g., Greenberg et al., 1990) and a striving to attain self-esteem (e.g., Routledge, Arndt, & Goldenberg, 2004; see Pyszczynski, Greenberg, Solomon, Arndt, & Schimel, 2004, for a review). Although terror management theory has traditionally focused on the effects of unconscious concerns with mortality on these symbolic or indirect distal defenses, recent research has led to the conceptualization of a dual defense model that also explicates responses provoked by conscious death-related thoughts (Arndt, Cook, & Routledge, 2004; Pyszczynski, Greenberg, & Solomon, 1999).[19]

   a. Is the theory adequately described? Explain.

[18] Elfenbein, H. A., Beaupré, M., Lévesque, M., & Hess, U. (2007). Toward a dialect theory: Cultural differences in the expression and recognition of posed facial expressions. *Emotion*, *7*, 131–146.

[19] Arndt, J., Cook, A., Goldenberg, J. L., & Cox, C. R. (2007). Cancer and the threat of death: The cognitive dynamics of death-thought suppression and its impact on behavioral health intentions. *Journal of Personality and Social Psychology*, *92*, 12–29.

5. An emergency medical condition is defined as a medical condition manifesting itself by acute symptoms of sufficient severity (including severe pain, psychiatric disturbances and/or symptoms of substance abuse) such that the absence of immediate medical attention could reasonably be expected to result in placing the health of the individual (or, with respect to a pregnant woman, the health of the woman or her unborn child) in serious jeopardy.[20]

   a. Is the conceptual definition adequate? Explain.

Part C

Directions: Read two research reports in academic journals on a topic of interest to you. Apply the evaluation questions in this chapter to their introductions, and select the one to which you have given the highest ratings. Bring it to class for discussion. Be prepared to discuss its strengths and weaknesses.

---

[20] Kunen, S., Niederhauser, R., Smith P. O., Morris, J. A., & Marx, B. D. (2005). Race disparities in psychiatric rates in emergency departments. *Journal of Consulting and Clinical Psychology*, *73*, 116–126.

Notes

Chapter 5

A Closer Look at Evaluating Literature Reviews

As indicated in the previous chapter, literature reviews usually are integrated into the researcher's introductory statements. In that chapter, the emphasis was on the functions of the introduction and the most salient characteristics of a literature review. This chapter explores the quality of literature reviews in more detail.

___ 1. Has the researcher avoided citing a large number of sources for a single point?

Very satisfactory 5 4 3 2 1 Very unsatisfactory ***or*** N/A I/I

Comment: As a rough rule, citing more than six sources for a single point is often inappropriate.

When there are many sources for a single point, two things can be done. First, the researcher can break them into two or more subgroups. For instance, those sources dealing with one population (such as children) might be cited in one group, while those sources dealing with another population (such as adolescents) might be cited in another group.

Second, the researcher can cite only selected sources as examples of the sources that support a point, which is illustrated in Example 5.1.1. Notice that the researchers make reference to "vast empirical literature," indicating that there are many sources that support the point. Then they use *e.g.,* (meaning "for example,") to cite two selected sources.

Example 5.1.1[1]

Using e.g., *to cite selected sources (bold added for emphasis)*:

A vast empirical literature has substantiated the existence of a link between symptoms of depression and marital conflict. Although this relationship is undoubtedly bidirectional and reciprocal (**e.g.,** Whisman, Uebelacker, & Weinstock, 2004), data suggest that the effect may be more strongly in the direction of depression leading to marital conflict (**e.g.,** Atkins, Dimidjian, Bedics, & Christensen, 2009).

---

[1] Marshall, A. D., Jones, D. E., & Feinberg, M. E. (2011). Enduring vulnerabilities, relationship attributions, and couple conflict: An integrative model of the occurrence and frequency of intimate partner violence. *Journal of Family Psychology, 25*, 709–718.

___ 2. Is the literature review critical?

Very satisfactory 5 4 3 2 1 Very unsatisfactory ***or*** N/A I/I

Comment: A researcher should consider the strengths and weaknesses of previously published studies.[2] Note that criticism can be positive (as in Example 5.2.1, in which the authors refer to "well-designed" studies).

Example 5.2.1[3]
Positive criticism in a literature review:

In the past 20 years, well-designed studies (e.g., those using more representative samples, clear exclusion criteria, subjects blind to study purpose, and standardized instruments) have challenged the view that children of alcoholics necessarily have poor psychosocial outcomes in adulthood. For example, Werner's (1986) pioneering longitudinal study of children born in Hawaii found differential effects of parental alcoholism in offspring, with 59% of the offspring reaching age 18 with no measureable adjustment problems. Clair and Genest (1987) showed that....

Of course, negative criticisms are often warranted. An instance of this is shown in Example 5.2.2.

Example 5.2.2[4]
Negative criticism in a literature review:

Nevertheless, several methodological limitations occurred in prior studies of parental involvement. An important limitation in these studies is one that is related to methodology; these studies focused on parental involvement as a whole but did not distinguish between mother's involvement and father's involvement (Flouri & Buchanan, 2004; Shek, 2007). The mother's influence on her child may be different from father's influence, as there are clear differences in how mother and father treat their children (McBride & Mills, 1993)....

A second limitation of research in this area is that, although a limited amount of research has been done to compare the different effects of father's involvement and mother's involvement, these studies used only infant or preschool children and did not include adolescents....

---

[2] Articles based on reasonably strong methodology may be cited without comments on their strengths. However, researchers have an obligation to point out which studies are exceptionally weak. This might be done with comments such as "A small pilot study suggested...."

[3] Amodeo, M., Griffin, M., & Paris, R. (2011). Women's reports of negative, neutral, and positive effects of growing up with alcoholic parents. *Families in Society: The Journal of Contemporary Social Services*, *92*, 69–76.

[4] Hsu, H.-Y., Zhang, D., Kwok, O.-M., Li, Y., & Ju, S. (2011). Distinguishing the influences of father's and mother's involvement on adolescent academic achievement: Analyses of Taiwan Educational Panel Survey Data. *Journal of Early Adolescence*, *31*, 694–713.

Another limitation of prior research is that parental involvement and the effect of such involvement on adolescent academic achievement is often confounded by ethnic and cultural factors....

___ 3. Is current research cited?

Very satisfactory 5 4 3 2 1 Very unsatisfactory ***or*** N/A I/I

Comment: The currency of the literature can be checked by noting whether research published in recent years has been cited. Keep in mind, however, that relevance to the research topic is more important than currency. A 10-year-old study that is highly relevant and has superior research methodology may deserve more attention than a less relevant, methodologically weaker one that was recently published. When this is the case, the researcher should explicitly state why an older research article is being discussed in more detail than newer ones.

Also, note that a researcher may want to cite older sources to establish the historical context for the study. In Example 5.3.1, the researchers link a particular finding to Ferster and Skinner's work in 1957. Skinner is the best known of the early behavior analysts. References to more current literature follow.

Example 5.3.1[5]

An excerpt from a literature review showing historical links:

Behavior analysts often allude to the imperviousness of schedule effects to particular reinforcement histories (e.g., Ferster & Skinner, 1957), but rarely is evidence adduced to substantiate that point. There is currently a small body of mixed evidence for reinforcement history effects on FI [fixed-interval] performance (Baron & Leinenweber, 1995; Cole, 2001....) For example, Wanchisen et al. (1989) found....

___ 4. Has the researcher distinguished between opinions and research findings?

Very satisfactory 5 4 3 2 1 Very unsatisfactory ***or*** N/A I/I

Comment: Researchers should use wording that helps readers understand whether the cited literature presents opinions or research results.

For indicating that a citation is research based, there is a variety of options, several of which are shown in Example 5.4.1.

---

[5] Ludvig, E. A., & Staddon, J. E. R. (2004). The conditions for temporal tracking under interval schedules of reinforcement. *Journal of Experimental Psychology: Animal Behavior Processes*, *30*, 299–316.

Example 5.4.1
Examples of key terms and expressions indicating that a citation is research based:

Recent data suggest that....

In laboratory experiments....

Recent test scores suggest....

Group A has outperformed its counterparts on measures of....

Research on XYZ has....

Data from surveys comparing....

Doe (2011) found that the rate....

These studies have greatly increased knowledge of....

The mean scores for women exceed....

The percentage of men who....

Note that if a researcher cites a specific statistic from the literature (e.g., "Approximately 22% of Canadian teenagers between 15 and 19 years currently smoke cigarettes [*Health Canada*, 2003].")[6], it is safe to assume that research is being cited.

Sometimes, researchers cite the opinions of others. When they do this, they should word their statements in such a way that readers are made aware that opinions (and not research findings) are being cited. Example 5.4.2 shows some examples of key words and phrases that researchers sometimes use to do this.

Example 5.4.2
Examples of key terms and expressions indicating that an opinion is being cited:

Jones (2010) has argued that....

These kinds of assumptions were....

Despite this speculation....

These arguments predict....

This logical suggestion....

Smith has strongly advocated the use of....

Based on the theory, (Smith, 2011) predicted that....

___ 5. Has the researcher noted any gaps in the literature?

Very satisfactory 5 4 3 2 1 Very unsatisfactory ***or*** N/A I/I

Comment: Gaps in the literature on a topic (areas not fully explored by researchers) can be as important as areas already explored by researchers. The gaps point to areas needing research in the future. In Example 5.5.1, the researchers point out a gap.

---

[6] As cited in Golmier, I., Chebat, J.-C., & Gelinas-Chebat, C. (2007). Can cigarette warnings counterbalance effects of smoking scenes in movies? *Psychological Reports*, *100*, 3–18.

Example 5.5.1[7]

Excerpt pointing out a gap in the literature:

Although the importance of fathers has been established, the majority of research on fathering is based on data from middle-class European American families, and research on ethnic minority fathers, especially Latino fathers, has lagged significantly behind (Cabrera & Garcia-Coll, 2004). This is a shortcoming of the literature....

Note that the presence of a gap in the literature can be used to justify a study when the purpose of the study is to fill the gap.

___ 6. Has the researcher interpreted research literature in light of the inherent limits of empirical research?

Very satisfactory 5 4 3 2 1 Very unsatisfactory ***or*** N/A I/I

Comment: As indicated in Chapter 1, empirical research has inherent limitations. As a result, no research report offers proof, and facts are very rarely revealed by empirical research. Instead, research results offer *degrees of evidence*, which are sometimes extremely strong (such as the relationship between cigarette smoking and health), and much more often are only modest or weak.

Terms that researchers might use to indicate that the results of research offer strong evidence are shown in Example 5.6.1.

Example 5.6.1

Examples of terminology (in bold) that can be used to indicate strong evidence:

Results of three recent studies **strongly suggest** that X and Y are....

Most studies of X and Y **clearly indicate the possibility** that X and Y are....

This type of evidence **has led most researchers to conclude** that X and Y....

Terms that researchers can use to indicate that the results of research offer moderate to weak evidence are shown in Example 5.6.2.

Example 5.6.2

Examples of terminology (in bold) that can be used to indicate moderate to weak evidence:

The results of a recent pilot study **suggest** that X and Y are....

To date, there is **only limited evidence** that X and Y are....

Although empirical evidence **is inconclusive**, X and Y seem to be....

Recent research **indicates** that X and Y....

---

[7] Cruz, R. A., King, K. M., Widaman, K. F., Leu, J., Cauce, A. M., & Conger, R. D. (2011). Cultural influences on positive father involvement in two-parent Mexican-origin families. *Journal of Family Psychology*, *25*, 731–740.

> The relationship between X and Y has been examined, with results **pointing toward**....

It is not necessary for a researcher to indicate the degree of confidence that should be accorded every finding discussed in a literature review. However, if a researcher merely states what the results of research indicate without qualifying terms, readers will assume that the research being cited is reasonably strong.

___ 7. Has the researcher avoided overuse of direct quotations from the literature?

Very satisfactory 5 4 3 2 1 Very unsatisfactory ***or*** N/A I/I

Comment: Direct quotations should be rarely used in literature reviews for two reasons. First, they often take up more journal space, which is very limited, than a paraphrase would take. Second, they often interrupt the flow of the text because of the differences in writing styles of the reviewer and the author of the literature.

An occasional quotation may be used if it expresses an idea or concept that would lose its impact in a paraphrase. This may be the case with a quotation shown in Example 5.7.1, which appeared in the first paragraph of a research report on drug abuse and its association with loneliness.

Example 5.7.1[8]

A direct quotation in a literature review (acceptable if done very sparingly):

> Recent studies suggest that a large proportion of the population are frequently lonely (Rokach & Brock, 1997). Ornish (1998) stated at the very beginning of his book *Love & Survival*: "Our survival depends on the healing power of love, intimacy, and relationships. Physically. Emotionally. Spiritually. As individuals. As communities. As a culture. Perhaps even as a species." (p. 1.) Indeed, loneliness has been linked to depression, anxiety and....

___ 8. Overall, is the literature review portion of the introduction appropriate?

Very satisfactory 5 4 3 2 1 Very unsatisfactory ***or*** N/A I/I

Comment: Rate this evaluation question after considering your answers to the earlier ones in this chapter and taking into account any additional considerations and concerns you may have. Be prepared to explain your overall evaluation.

---

[8] Orzeck, T., & Rokach, A. (2004). Men who abuse drugs and their experience of loneliness. *European Psychologist*, *9*, 163–169.

Exercise for Chapter 5

Part A

Directions: Answer the following questions.

1. Consider Statement A and Statement B. They both contain the same citations. In your opinion, which statement is superior? Explain.

   Statement A: The overall positive association between nonverbal decoding skills and workplace effectiveness has been replicated with adults in a variety of settings (Campbell, Kagan, & Krathwohl, 1971; Costanzo & Philpott, 1986; Schag, Loo, & Levin, 1978; DiMatteo, Friedman, & Taranta, 1979; Tickle-Degnen, 1998; Halberstadt & Hall, 1980; Izard, 1971; Izard et al., 2001; Nowicki & Duke, 1994).

   Statement B: The overall positive association between nonverbal decoding skills and workplace effectiveness has been replicated with adults in counseling settings (Campbell, Kagan, & Krathwohl, 1971; Costanzo & Philpott, 1986; Schag, Loo, & Levin, 1978) and medical settings (DiMatteo, Friedman, & Taranta, 1979; Tickle-Degnen, 1998), and with children in academic settings (Halberstadt & Hall, 1980; Izard, 1971; Izard et al., 2001; Nowicki & Duke, 1994).[9]

2. Consider Statement C. This statement could have been used as an example for which evaluation question in this chapter?

   Statement C: In contrast to the somewhat sizable body of research informing secular program practice to reduce relapse and recidivism, the literature on faith-based religious programming has produced very few outcome-based studies. With regard to community-based corrections-related programming, evaluations are almost nonexistent.[10]

3. Consider Statement D. This statement could have been used as an example for which evaluation question in this chapter?

   Statement D: Research on happiness and subjective well-being has generated many intriguing findings, among which is that happiness is context dependent and relative (e.g., Brickman & Campbell, 1971; Easterlin, 1974, 2001; Parducci, 1995; Ubel, Loewenstein, & Jepson, 2005; see Diener et al., 2006; Hsee & Has-

---

[9] Effenbein, H. A., & Ambady, N. (2002). Predicting workplace outcomes from the ability to eavesdrop on feelings. *Journal of Applied Psychology*, *87*, 963–971.

[10] Roman, C. G., Wolff, A., Correa, V., & Buck, J. (2007). Assessing intermediate outcomes of a faith-based residential prisoner reentry program. *Research on Social Work Practice*, *17*, 199–215.

tie, 2006, for reviews). For example, paraplegics can be nearly as happy as lottery winners (Brickman et al., 1978). However, to assess happiness....[11]

4. Consider Statement E. This statement could have been used as an example for which evaluation question in this chapter?

    Statement E: When speaking of "help-seeking" behaviors or patterns, Rogler and Cortes (1993) proposed that "from the beginning, psychosocial and cultural factors impinge upon the severity and type of mental health problems; these factors [thus] interactively shape the [help-seeking] pathways' direction and duration" (p. 556).[12]

5. Consider Statement F. This statement could have been used as an example for which evaluation question in this chapter?

    Statement F: In the majority of studies referred to above, the findings have been correlational in nature, with the result that it has not been possible to draw causal inferences between low cortisol concentrations and antisocial behavior.[13]

Part B

Directions: Read the introductions to three research reports in academic journals on a topic of interest to you. Apply the evaluation questions in this chapter to the literature reviews in their introductions, and select the one to which you gave the highest ratings. Bring it to class for discussion. Be prepared to discuss its specific strengths and weaknesses.

[11] Hsee, C. K., & Tang, J. N. (2007). Sun and water: On a modulus-based measurement of happiness. *Emotion*, *7*, 213–218.

[12] Akutsu, P. D., Castillo, E. D., & Snowden, L. R. (2007). Differential referral patterns to ethnic-specific and mainstream mental health programs for four Asian American groups. *American Journal of Orthopsychiatry*, *77*, 95–103.

[13] van Goozen, S. H. M., Fairchild, G., Snoek, H., & Harold, G. T. (2007). The evidence for a neurobiological model of childhood antisocial behavior. *Psychological Bulletin*, *133*, 149–182.

Chapter 6

Evaluating Samples When Researchers Generalize

Immediately after the introduction, which includes a literature review, most researchers insert the main heading of Method. In the Method section, researchers almost always begin by describing the individuals they studied. This description is usually prefaced with one of these subheadings: Subjects or Participants. [1]

A *population* is any group in which a researcher is ultimately interested. It might be large, such as all registered voters in Pennsylvania, or it might be small, such as all members of a local teachers' association. Researchers often study only *samples* (i.e., a subset of a population) for the sake of efficiency, then *generalize* their results to the population of interest. In other words, they infer that the data they collected by studying samples are similar to the data they would have obtained by studying the entire populations.

Because many researchers do not explicitly state whether they are attempting to generalize, consumers of research often need to make a judgment on this matter in order to decide whether to apply the evaluation questions in this chapter to the research report being evaluated. To make this decision, consider these questions:

Does the researcher *imply* that the results apply to some larger population?

Does the researcher discuss the implications of his or her research for a larger group of individuals than the one directly studied?

If the answers are clearly "yes," apply the evaluation questions in this chapter to the article being evaluated. Note that the evaluation of samples when researchers are clearly *not* attempting to generalize to populations is considered in the next chapter.

___ 1. Was random sampling used?

Very satisfactory 5 4 3 2 1 Very unsatisfactory ***or*** N/A I/I

Comment: Using random sampling (like drawing names out of a hat) yields an *unbiased* sample (i.e., a sample that does not systematically favor any particular type of individual or group in the selection process). If a sample is unbiased and reasonably large, researchers are likely to make sound generalizations. (Sample size will be discussed later in this chapter.)

---

[1] The term *participant* indicates that the individuals being studied have consented to participate after being informed of the nature of the research project, its potential benefits, and its potential harm. In contrast, the term *subjects* is preferred when there is no consent—such as in animal studies.

The desirability of using random sampling as the basis for making generalizations is so widely recognized among researchers that they are almost certain to mention its use if it was employed in selecting samples. Example 6.1.1 shows three instances of how this has recently been expressed in published research.

Example 6.1.1

Brief description of the use of random sampling in three research articles:

Surveys were sent to 600 psychologists who were randomly selected from a list of 872 licensed psychologists who were members of the Illinois Psychological Association.[2]

A random national sample composed of 681 licensed practicing psychologists who are members of the American Psychological Association's Division 20 (Adult Development and Aging) was surveyed regarding assessment and treatment of suicide risk in older adult patients and perception of risk factors for completed suicide among older adults.[3]

Participants were randomly sampled by household address from Colorado's general population....[4]

___ 2. If random sampling was used, was it stratified?

Very satisfactory 5 4 3 2 1 Very unsatisfactory ***or*** N/A I/I

Comment: Researchers use *stratified random sampling* by drawing individuals separately at random from different strata (i.e., subgroups) within a population. For instance, suppose a researcher wants to survey licensed clinical psychologists in a large city. To stratify, the researcher might divide the population into four subgroups: those who practice on the north side of town, those who practice on the east side, and so on. Then he or she could draw a fixed percentage at random from each side of town. The result will be a sample that is geographically representative. For instance, if 40% of the population practices on the west side, then 40% of the sample will be from the west side.

Stratifying will improve a sample only if the stratification variable (e.g., geography) is related to the variables to be studied. For instance, if the researcher is planning to study how psychologists work with illicit substance abusers, stratifying on geography will improve the sample if the various areas of the city tend to have different types of drug problems, which may require different treatment modalities.

---

[2] Stevanovic, P., & Rupert, P. A. (2004). Career-sustaining behaviors, satisfactions, and stresses of professional psychologists. *Psychotherapy: Theory, Research, Practice, Training*, *41*, 301–309.

[3] Brown, L. M., Bongar, B., & Cleary, K. M. (2004). A profile of psychologists' views of critical risk factors for completed suicide in older adults. *Professional Psychology: Research and Practice*, *35*, 90–96.

[4] Plant, E. A., & Sachs-Ericsson, N. (2004). Racial and ethnic differences in depression: The roles of social support and meeting basic needs. *Journal of Consulting and Clinical Psychology*, *72*, 41–52.

Note that geography is often an excellent variable on which to stratify because people tend to cluster geographically on the basis of many variables that are important in the social and behavioral sciences. For instance, they often cluster according to race/ethnicity, income/personal wealth, language preference, religion, and so on. Thus, a geographically representative sample is likely to be representative in terms of these other variables as well. Other common stratification variables are occupation, highest educational level attained, political affiliation, and age.

In Example 6.2.1, geography was used as a stratification variable.

Example 6.2.1[5]

Description of the use of stratified random sampling:

The data for our investigation came from a survey of 3,690 seventh-grade students from 65 middle schools in randomly selected counties in the state of Kentucky. Four strata were used: (1) counties with a minimum population of 150,000, (2) counties with population sizes between 40,000 and 150,000, (3) counties with population sizes between 15,000 and 40,000, and (4) counties with population sizes below 15,000.

If random sampling without stratification is used, the technique is called *simple random sampling*. In contrast, if stratification is used to form subgroups from which random samples are drawn, the technique is called *stratified random sampling.*

Despite the almost universal acceptance that an unbiased sample obtained through simple or stratified random sampling is highly desirable for making generalizations, the vast majority of research from which researchers want to make generalizations is based on studies in which nonrandom (biased) samples were used. There are three major reasons for this:

1. Even though a random selection of names might have been drawn, a researcher often cannot convince all those selected to participate in the research project. This problem is addressed in the next three evaluation questions.
2. Many researchers have limited resources with which to conduct research: limited time, money, and assistance. Often, they will reach out to individuals who are readily accessible or convenient to use as participants. For instance, college professors conducting research often find that the most convenient samples consist of students enrolled in their classes, which are not even random samples of students on their campuses. This is called *convenience sampling*, which is a highly suspect method for drawing samples from which to generalize.
3. For some populations, it is difficult to identify all members. If a researcher cannot do this, he or she obviously cannot draw a random sample of the entire population. Examples of populations whose members are difficult to identify are the homeless

[5] This example is loosely based on the work of Ousey, G. C., & Wilcox, P. (2005). Subcultural values and violent delinquency: A multilevel analysis in middle schools. *Youth Violence and Juvenile Justice*, *3*, 3–22.

in a large city, successful burglars (i.e., those who have never been caught), and illicit drug users.

Because so many researchers study nonrandom samples, it is unrealistic to count failures on the first two evaluation questions in this chapter as fatal flaws in research methodology. If journal editors routinely refused to publish research reports with this type of deficiency, there would be very little published research on many of the most important problems in the social and behavioral sciences. Thus, when researchers use nonrandom samples when attempting to generalize, the additional evaluation questions raised in this chapter should be applied in order to distinguish between studies from which it is reasonable to make tentative, very cautious generalizations and those that are hopelessly flawed with respect to their sampling.

___ 3. If some potential participants refused to participate, was the rate of participation reasonably high?

Very satisfactory 5 4 3 2 1 Very unsatisfactory ***or*** N/A I/I

Comment: Defining *reasonably high* is problematic. For instance, a professional survey organization, with trained personnel and substantial resources, would be concerned if it had a response rate of less than 80% when conducting a national survey. On the other hand, researchers with limited resources using mailed questionnaires often are satisfied with a return rate as low as 50%, especially because rates of returns to mailed surveys are notoriously poor. As a very rough rule of thumb, then, response rates of substantially less than 50% raise serious concerns about the generalizability of the findings.

Example 6.3.1 reports a reasonable response rate for a mailed survey.

Example 6.3.1[6]

Reasonable response rates for a mailed survey:

Surveys returned without forwarding addresses, for deceased respondents, or those with incomplete responses were eliminated from the sample. The response rates were 56.7% psychologists (*n* = 603), 45.8% psychiatrists (*n* = 483), and 58.2% social workers (*n* = 454), resulting in a 53% overall survey response rate and a total sample (*N* = 1,540).

The percentages mentioned above should not be applied mechanically during research evaluation because exceptions may be made for cases in which participation in the research is burdensome or invasive or raises sensitive issues—factors that might make it understandable to obtain a lower rate of participation. For instance, if a researcher needed to draw samples of blood from students on campus to estimate the incidence of a certain type of infection or needed to put a sample of students through a

[6] Pottick, K. J., Kirk, S. A., Hsieh, D. K., & Tian, X. (2007). Judging mental disorder in youths: Effects of client, clinical, and contextual differences. *Journal of Consulting and Clinical Psychology*, *75*, 1–8.

series of rigorous physical fitness tests that spanned several days for a study in sports psychology, a consumer of research might judge a participation rate of substantially less than 50% to be reasonable in light of the particulars of the research, keeping in mind that any generalizations to populations would be highly tenuous.

___ 4. If the response rate was low, did the researcher make multiple attempts to contact potential participants?

Very satisfactory 5 4 3 2 1 Very unsatisfactory ***or*** N/A I/I

Comment: Researchers often make multiple attempts to contact potential participants. For instance, a researcher might contact potential participants several times (e.g., by several mailings and by phone) and still achieve a response rate of less than 50%. In this case, a consumer of research might reach the conclusion that this is the highest rate of return that might be expected for the researcher's particular research problem and population. In effect, the consumer might judge that this is the best that can be done, keeping in mind that generalizations from such a sample are exceedingly risky because nonparticipants might be fundamentally different from those who agreed to participate.

Example 6.4.1 describes multiple contacts made by researchers in an effort to achieve a high response rate.

Example 6.4.1[7]

Multiple attempts to obtain a sample:

Potential participants were first contacted with an e-mail invitation that included a link to complete the online survey. This was followed by up to 5 reminder e-mails sent by the survey center and up to 10 attempted follow-up telephone contacts as needed. The telephone calls served as a reminder to complete the survey online and an opportunity to complete the survey over the phone. Only 3 of our respondents chose to complete the survey over the phone versus online.

___ 5. Is there reason to believe that the participants and nonparticipants are similar on relevant variables?

Very satisfactory 5 4 3 2 1 Very unsatisfactory ***or*** N/A I/I

Comment: In some instances, researchers have information about those who do not participate, which allows for a comparison of nonparticipants with participants. For instance, a researcher might note the zip codes on the envelopes in which returned ques-

[7] Winters, K. C., Toomey, T., Nelson, T. F., Erickson, D., Lenk, K., & Miazga, M. (2011). Screening for alcohol problems among 4-year colleges and universities. *Journal of American College Health, 59*, 350–357.

tionnaires were posted. This might allow a researcher to determine whether those in affluent neighborhoods were more responsive than those in less affluent ones.[8]

In institutional settings such as schools, hospitals, and prisons, it is often possible to determine whether participants and nonparticipants differ in important respects. For instance, in a survey regarding political attitudes held by college students, participants might be asked for background information such as major, GPA, and age. These background characteristics are usually known for the population of students on the campus, allowing for a comparison of participants and the entire student body. If there are substantial differences, the results will need to be interpreted in light of them. For instance, if political science majors were a much larger percentage of the participants than exists in the whole student body, the researcher should be highly cautious in generalizing the results to all students.

In the evaluation of a new component for the Head Start program in rural areas of Oregon, only 56% agreed to participate. However, the researchers noted the similarities of these participants with the general population in Example 6.5.1. This provides some assurance that those who chose to participate in the research were not substantially different from nonparticipants in terms of important background characteristics (i.e., demographics).

Example 6.5.1[9]

Comparison of a flawed sample with a larger group:

Forty-five percent of children [were] living in families including both biological parents. Sixty percent of the children and families received public assistance. Eighty-three percent were Caucasian, and 13% were other ethnic groups, primarily Hispanic. These demographics are representative of the rural population in Oregon.

___ 6. If a sample is not random, was it at least drawn from the target group for the generalization?

Very satisfactory 5 4 3 2 1 Very unsatisfactory ***or*** N/A I/I

Comment: There are many instances in the published literature in which a researcher studied one type of participant (e.g., college freshmen) and used the data to make generalizations to a different target group (e.g., young adults in general).[10] If a researcher

---

[8] If such a bias were detected, statistical adjustments might be made to correct for it by mathematically giving more weight to the respondents from the underrepresented zip codes.

[9] Kaminski, R. A., Stormshak, E. A., Good, R. H. III, & Goodman, M. R. (2002). Prevention of substance abuse with rural Head Start children and families: Results of Project STAR. *Psychology of Addictive Behaviors*, *16*, S11–S26.

[10] In this context, it is interesting to note that the editor of the *Journal of Adolescent Research* pointed out that "Many articles currently published in journals on adolescence are based on American middle-class samples but draw conclusions about adolescents in general." (p. 5). Arnett, J. J. (2005). The vitality criterion: A new standard of publication for *Journal of Adolescent Research*. *Journal of Adolescent Research*, *20*, 3–7.

does not have the wherewithal to at least tap into the target group of interest, it might be better to leave the research to other researchers who have the resources and contacts that give them access to members of the target group.

Example 6.6.1 describes the convenience sample (nonrandom) used in a study on the provision of mental health services to college students. The researchers wanted to apply the results only to college students. Thus, the sample is adequate in terms of this evaluation question because the sample was drawn from the target group.

Example 6.6.1[11]

Nonrandom sample from the target group (college students):

Three hundred students (201 women, 98 men, 1 not indicating gender) enrolled in introductory college courses served as participants. Students were at least age 18, attending a medium-sized state university in the Midwestern United States. Participants were recruited from their university's multidepartment research pool (n = 546) for research or extra credit through a password-protected Web site listing available university-specific studies for electronic sign-up.

___ 7. If a sample is not random, was it drawn from diverse sources?

Very satisfactory 5 4 3 2 1 Very unsatisfactory ***or*** N/A I/I

Comment: Did a researcher generalize to all college students after studying only students attending a small religious college in which 99% of the students have the same ethnic/racial background? Did a researcher generalize to men and women regarding the relationship between exercise and health after studying only men attending a cardiac unit's exercise program? An answer of "yes" to these types of questions might lead to a low rating for this evaluation question.

When a researcher wants to generalize to a larger population in the absence of random sampling, consider whether a researcher sought participants from several sources, which increases the odds of representativeness. For instance, much educational research is conducted in just one school. Using students from several schools within the district would increase the odds that the resulting sample will reflect the diversity of the district.

In Example 6.7.1, the researchers used three methods for drawing a sample for a study of parents with disabilities. This is vastly superior to using just one method for locating participants in a hard-to-reach population.

---

[11] Elhai, J. D., & Simons, J. S. (2007). Trauma exposure and posttraumatic stress disorder predictors of mental health treatment use in college students. *Psychological Services*, *4*, 38–45.

Example 6.7.1[12]

Diverse sources for a sample:

We used three avenues for recruitment of parents with disabilities. The first was to distribute survey packets to many disability organizations and service agencies and to ask them to distribute the survey packets. There are drawbacks to this method. ...This distribution method solicits responses only from families connected to a disability or service agency in some way. Such families may differ from those with no connections to such agencies.

The second method was to solicit participants directly by placing announcements and ads in many different venues and having interested parents call us for a survey. This was our primary recruitment method. Contact was made with 548 agencies, resulting in announcements or ads in newsletters or other publications associated with those agencies.

The third method of outreach was through the Internet. E-mail and Web site postings went to agencies serving people with disabilities, parents, and/or children, as well as bulletin boards, and were updated frequently. Approximately 650 Web sites were visited and requested to help distribute information about this survey. Additionally, we investigated 65 electronic mailing lists and subscribed to 27. Last, we purchased a list of addresses, phone numbers, and e-mail addresses of various disability-related agencies, magazines, and newsletters. We contacted these sites by phone and followed up with an informational e-mail.

___ 8. If a sample is not random, does the researcher explicitly discuss this limitation?

Very satisfactory 5 4 3 2 1 Very unsatisfactory ***or*** N/A I/I

Comment: While researchers may discuss the limitations of their methodology (including sampling) in any part of their reports, many explicitly discuss limitations in the Discussion section at the end of their reports. Example 6.8.1 appeared near the end of a research report.

Example 6.8.1[13]

Statement of a limitation in sampling:

The limited number and geographic location (rural eastern North Carolina) of the churches in this study may not be generalizable to other types of churches, other population groups, or other geographic areas.

Example 6.8.2 is an acknowledgment of a sampling limitation that appeared as the last few sentences in a research report.

---

[12] Olkin, R., Abrams, K., Preston, P., & Kirshbaum, M. (2006). Comparison of parents with and without disabilities raising teens: Information from the NHIS and two national surveys. *Rehabilitation Psychology, 51*, 43–49.

[13] Campbell, M. K., James, A., Hudson, M. A., Carr, C., Jackson, E., Oakes, V., ... Tessaro, I. (2004). Improving multiple behaviors for colorectal cancer prevention among African American church members. *Health Psychology, 23*, 492–502.

Example 6.8.2[14]

Statement of a limitation in sampling:

Finally, the fact that patients with a lifetime history of psychotic disorder, or alcohol or drug addiction, were not included in the study may have biased the sample, limiting the generalizability of the findings. The results should be treated with caution, and replication, preferably including a larger sample size, is recommended.

Such acknowledgments of limitations do not improve researchers' ability to generalize. However, they do perform two important functions: (a) They serve as warnings to naïve readers regarding the problem of generalizing, and (b) they reassure all readers that the researchers are aware of a serious flaw in their methodology.

___ 9. Has the author described relevant demographics of the sample?

Very satisfactory 5 4 3 2 1 Very unsatisfactory ***or*** N/A I/I

Comment: A researcher should describe the relevant demographics (i.e., background characteristics). For instance, when studying physicians' attitudes toward assisted suicide, it would be relevant to know their religious affiliations. For studying consumers' preferences, it would be helpful to know their economic status.

In addition to demographics that are directly relevant to the variables being studied, it usually is desirable to provide an overall demographic profile, including variables such as age, gender, race/ethnicity, and highest level of education. This is especially important when a nonrandom sample of convenience has been used because readers will want to visualize the particular participants who were part of such a sample.

Example 6.9.1 is from a study on stress in nurses who provide palliative care for terminally ill patients.

Example 6.9.1[15]

Description of relevant demographics:

The sample included 209 nurses. They reported spending, on average, 20% of their working time in palliative care and had been working in this area for at least two years. The participants worked in community- (52%) or hospital-based (47%) palliative care settings. Most nurses were females (92.3%; males: 7.7%) and employed full-time (54.5%; part-time: 25.4%; occasional: 12.4%; other: 7.7%). The nurses' mean age was 43 (*SD* = 9.01), with an average of 16 years

---

[14] Chioqueta, A. P., & Stiles, T. C. (2004). Suicide risk in patients with somatization disorder. *Crisis: The Journal of Crisis Intervention and Suicide*, *25*, 3–7.

[15] Fillion, L. et al. (2007). Job satisfaction and emotional distress among nurses providing palliative care: Empirical evidence for an integrative occupational stress-model. *International Journal of Stress Management*, *14*, 1–25.

(*SD* = 1.86) of education, and an average of 19 years (*SD* = 9.12) of experience as a nurse.

When a large number of demographics have been collected, researchers often present them in statistical tables instead of in the narrative of the report.

___ 10. Is the overall size of the sample adequate?

Very satisfactory 5 4 3 2 1 Very unsatisfactory ***or*** N/A I/I

Comment: Students who are new to research methods are sometimes surprised to learn that there often is no simple answer to the question of how large a sample should be. First, it depends in part on how much error a researcher is willing to tolerate. For public opinion polls, a stratified random sample of about 1,500 produces a margin of error of about one to three percentage points. A sample size of 400 produces a margin of error of about four to six percentage points.[16] If a researcher is trying to predict the outcome of a close election, clearly a sample size of 400 would be inadequate.[17]

Responding to a public opinion poll usually takes little time and may be of interest to many participants. Other types of studies, however, may be of less interest to potential participants and/or may require extensive effort on the part of participants. In addition, certain data-collection methods (such as individual interviews) may require expenditure of considerable resources by researchers. Under such circumstances, it may be unrealistic to expect a researcher to use large samples. Thus, a consumer of research should ask whether the researchers used a reasonable number given the particular circumstances of their studies. Would it have been an unreasonable burden to use substantially more participants? Is the number of participants so low that there is little hope of making sound generalizations? Would it be reasonable to base an important decision on the results of the study given the number of participants used? Subjective answers to these types of questions will guide consumers of research on this evaluation question.[18]

It is important to keep in mind that a large sample size does not compensate for a bias in sampling due to the failure to use random sampling. Using large numbers of unrepresentative participants does not get around the problem of their unrepresentativeness.

---

[16] The exact size of the margin of error depends on whether the sample was stratified and on other sampling issues that are beyond the scope of this book.

[17] With a sample of only 400 individuals, there would need to be an 8 to 12 percentage-point *difference* (twice the four- to six-point margin of error) between the two candidates for a reliable prediction to be made (i.e., a statistically significant prediction).

[18] There are statistical methods for estimating optimum sample sizes under various assumptions. While these methods are beyond the scope of this book, note that they do not take into account the practical matters raised here.

___11. Is the number of participants in each subgroup sufficiently large?

Very satisfactory 5 4 3 2 1 Very unsatisfactory ***or*** N/A I/I

Comment: Consider the hypothetical information in Example 6.11.1, where the numbers of participants in each subgroup are indicated by *n*, and the mean (average) scores are indicated by *m*.

Example 6.11.1

A sample in which some subgroups are very small:

A random sample of 100 college freshmen was surveyed on its knowledge of alcoholism. The mean (*m*) scores out of a maximum of 25 were as follows: White (m = 18.5, n = 78), African American (m = 20.1, n = 11), Hispanic/Latino (m = 19.9, n = 9), and Chinese American (m = 17.9, n = 2). Thus, for each of the four ethnic/racial groups, there was a reasonably high average knowledge of alcoholism.

Although the total number in the sample is 100 (a number that might be acceptable for some research purposes), the numbers of participants in the last three subgroups in Example 6.11.1 are so small that it would be highly inappropriate to generalize from them to their respective populations. The researcher should either obtain larger numbers of them or refrain from reporting separately on the individual subgroups. Notice that there is nothing wrong with indicating ethnic/racial backgrounds (such as the fact that there were two Chinese American participants) in describing the demographics of the sample. Instead, the problem is that the number of individuals in some of the subgroups is too small to justify calculating a mean and making an inference about them. For instance, a mean of 17.9 for the Chinese Americans is meaningless for the purpose of generalizing because there are only two individuals in this subgroup.

___12. Has informed consent been obtained?

Very satisfactory 5 4 3 2 1 Very unsatisfactory ***or*** N/A I/I

Comment: It is almost always highly desirable to obtain written, informed consent from the participants in a study. Participants should be informed of the nature of the study and, at least in general terms, the nature of their involvement. They should also be informed of their right to withdraw from the study at any time without penalty. Typically, researchers report only very briefly on this matter, as illustrated in Example 6.12.1, which presents a statement similar to many found in research reports in academic journals. It is unrealistic to expect much more detail than shown here because, by convention, the discussion of this issue is typically brief.

Example 6.12.1

Brief description of informed consent:

Students from the departmental subject pool volunteered to participate in this study for course credit. Prior to participating in the study, students were given an

> informed consent form that had been approved by the university's institutional review board. The form described the experiment as "a study of social interactions between male and female students" and informed them that if they consented, they were free to withdraw from the study at any time without penalty.

There may be times when a consumer of research judges that the study is so innocuous that informed consent might not be needed. An example is an observational study in which individuals are observed in public places, such as a public park or shopping mall, while the observers are in plain view. Because public behaviors are being observed by researchers in such instances, privacy would not normally be expected, and informed consent may not be required. Even for such studies, however, approval from a review board (such as a campus committee) should be obtained.

___ 13. Overall, is the sample appropriate for generalizing?

Very satisfactory 5 4 3 2 1 Very unsatisfactory ***or*** N/A I/I

Comment: Rate this evaluation question after considering your answers to the earlier ones in this chapter and taking into account any additional considerations and concerns you may have. Be prepared to discuss your response to this evaluation question.

Concluding Comment

Although a primary goal of much research in all the sciences is to make sound generalizations from samples to populations, researchers in the social and behavioral sciences face special problems regarding access to and cooperation from samples of humans. Unlike other published lists of criteria for evaluating samples, the criteria discussed in this chapter urge consumers of research to be pragmatic when making these evaluations. A researcher may exhibit some relatively serious flaws in sampling, yet a consumer may conclude that the researcher did a reasonable job under the circumstances. However, this does not preclude the need to be exceedingly cautious in making generalizations from studies with weak samples. Confidence in certain generalizations based on weak samples can be increased, however, if various researchers with different patterns of weaknesses in their sampling methods arrive at similar conclusions when studying the same research problems.

In the next chapter, the evaluation of samples when researchers do *not* attempt to generalize is considered.

Exercise for Chapter 6

Part A

Directions: Answer the following questions.

1. Suppose a researcher conducted a survey on a college campus by interviewing students that she or he approached while they were having dinner in the campus cafeteria one evening. In your opinion, is this a random sample of all students enrolled in the college? Could the method be improved? How?

2. Briefly explain why *geography* is often an excellent variable on which to stratify when sampling.

3. According to this chapter, the vast majority of research is based on biased samples. Cite one reason that is given in this chapter for this circumstance.

4. If multiple attempts have been made to contact potential participants, and yet the response rate is low, would you be willing to give the report a reasonably high rating for sampling? Explain.

5. Is it important to know whether participants and nonparticipants are similar on relevant variables? Explain.

6. Does the use of a large sample compensate for a bias in sampling? Explain.

Part B

Directions: Locate several research reports in academic journals in which the researchers are concerned with generalizing from a sample to a population, and apply the evaluation questions in this chapter. Select the one to which you gave the highest overall rating and bring it to class for discussion. Be prepared to discuss the strengths and weaknesses of the sampling method used.

Notes

Chapter 7

Evaluating Samples When Researchers Do *Not* Generalize

As indicated in the previous chapter, researchers often study samples in order to make inferences about the populations from which the samples were drawn. This process is known as generalizing.

Not all research is aimed at generalizing. Here are the major reasons why:

1. Researchers often conduct *pilot studies*. These are designed to determine the feasibility of methods for studying specific research problems. For instance, a novice researcher who wants to conduct an interview study of the social dynamics of marijuana use among high school students might conduct a pilot study to determine, among other things, how much cooperation can be obtained from school personnel for such a study, what percentage of the parents give permission for their children to participate in interviews on this topic, whether students have difficulty understanding the interview questions and whether they are willing to answer them, the optimum length of the interviews, and so on. After the research techniques are refined in a pilot study with a sample of convenience, a more definitive study with a more appropriate sample for generalizing might be conducted.

   Note that it is not uncommon for journals to publish reports of pilot studies, especially if they yield interesting results and point to promising directions for future research. Also note that while many researchers will explicitly identify their pilot studies as such (by using the term *pilot study*), at other times consumers of research will need to infer that a study is a pilot study from statements such as "The findings from this preliminary investigation suggest that...."

2. Some researchers focus on *developing and testing theories*. A theory is a proposition or set of propositions that provides a cohesive explanation of the underlying dynamics of certain aspects of behavior. For instance, self-verification theory indicates that people attempt to maintain stable self-concepts. On the basis of this theory, researchers can make a number of predictions. For instance, if the theory is correct, a researcher might predict that people with poor self-concepts will seek out negative social reinforcement (e.g., seek out people who give them negative feedback about themselves) while avoiding or rejecting positive reinforcement. They do not do this because they enjoy negative reinforcement. Instead, according to the theory, it is an attempt to validate their

perceptions of themselves.[1] Such predictions can be tested with empirical research, which sheds light on the validity of a theory, as well as data that may be used to further develop and refine it.

In addition to testing whether the predictions made on the basis of a theory are supported by data, researchers conduct studies to determine under what circumstances the elements of a theory hold up (e.g., in intimate relationships only? with mildly as well as severely depressed patients?). One researcher might test one aspect of the theory with a convenience sample of adolescent boys who are being treated for depression, another might test a different aspect with a convenience sample of high-achieving women, and so on. Note that they are focusing on the theory as an evolving concept rather than as a static explanation that needs to be tested with a random sample for generalization to a population. These studies may be viewed as *developmental tests* of a theory. For *preliminary* developmental work of this type, rigorous and expensive sampling from a large population usually is not justified.

3. Some researchers prefer to study *purposive samples* rather than random samples. A purposive sample is one in which a researcher has a special interest because the individuals in a sample have characteristics that make them especially rich sources of information. For instance, an anthropologist who is interested in studying tribal religious practices might purposively select a tribe that has remained isolated and, hence, may have been less influenced by outside religions than other tribes that are less isolated. Note that the tribe is not selected at random but is selected deliberately (i.e., purposively). The use of purposive samples is a tradition in *qualitative* research. (See Appendix A for a brief overview of the differences between qualitative and quantitative research.)

4. Some researchers study entire populations—not samples. This is especially true in institutional settings such as schools, where all the seniors in a school district (the population) might be tested. Nevertheless, when researchers write research reports on population studies, they should describe their populations in some detail.

___ 1. Has the researcher described the sample/population in sufficient detail?

Very satisfactory 5 4 3 2 1 Very unsatisfactory ***or*** N/A I/I

Comment: As indicated in the previous chapter, researchers should describe relevant demographics (i.e., background characteristics) of the participants when conducting studies in which they are generalizing from a sample to a population. This is also true when researchers are not attempting to generalize.

---

[1] For more information on this theory and its potential application to a particular behavioral issue, see Trouilloud, D., Sarrazin, P., Bressoux, P., & Bois, J. (2006). Relation between teachers' early expectations and students' later perceived competence in physical education classes: Autonomy-supportive climate as a moderator. *Journal of Educational Psychology, 98*, 75–86.

Example 7.1.1 shows a description of demographics from a qualitative research report in which the researchers are seeking in-depth information about a group of women living in a shelter because of domestic violence. The description of the demographics helps consumers of research "see" the participants, which makes the results of the study more meaningful.

Example 7.1.1[2]

Detailed description of the demographics of participants:

Ten participants were recruited from the local domestic violence shelter. They ranged in age from 20 to 47 years ($M = 35.4$, $SD = 7.5$). All 10 participants were women. Of the participants, 5 (50%) were Native American, 4 (40%) were European American, and 1 (10%) was Latina. Two (20%) participants were married, 2 (20%) were divorced, 2 (20%) were single, and 4 (40%) were separated from their spouses. Nine of the 10 (90%) participants had children, and the children's ages ranged from under 1 year to over 27 years. Educational levels included 5 (50%) participants who had taken some college or technical courses, 2 (20%) participants with a high school diploma or general equivalency diploma (GED), 1 participant (10%) with a 10th-grade education, 1 participant (10%) with a technical school degree, and 1 participant (10%) who was a doctoral candidate. Four participants were unemployed, 2 worked as secretaries, 1 worked as a waitress, 1 worked as a housekeeper, 1 worked in a local retail store, and 1 worked in a factory. Each participant listed a series of short-term, low-pay positions such as convenience store clerk.

___ **2. For a pilot study or developmental test of a theory, has the researcher used a sample with relevant demographics?**

Very satisfactory 5 4 3 2 1 Very unsatisfactory ***or*** N/A I/I

Comment: Studies that often fail on this evaluation question are those in which college students are used as participants (for convenience in sampling). For instance, some researchers have stretched the limits of credulity by conducting studies in which college students are asked to respond to questions that are unrelated to their life experiences, such as asking unmarried, childless college women what disciplinary measures they would take if they discovered that their hypothetical teenage sons were using illicit drugs. Obviously, posing such hypothetical questions to an inappropriate sample might yield little relevant information even in a pilot study.

Less extreme examples are frequently found in published research literature. For instance, using college students in tests of learning theories when the theories were constructed to explain the learning behavior of children would be inappropriate. When

[2] Wettersten, K. B., Rudolph, S. E., Faul, K., Gallagher, K., Trangsrud, H. B., Adams, K., ... Terrance, C. (2004). Freedom through self-sufficiency: A qualitative examination of the impact of domestic violence on the working lives of women in shelter. *Journal of Counseling Psychology*, *51*, 447–462.

applying this evaluation question to such studies, make some allowance for minor "misfits" between the sample used in a pilot study (or developmental test of a theory) and the population of ultimate interest. Keep in mind that pilot studies are not designed to provide definitive data—only preliminary information that will assist in refining future research.

___ 3. Even if the purpose is not to generalize to a population, has the researcher used a sample of adequate size?

Very satisfactory 5 4 3 2 1 Very unsatisfactory ***or*** N/A I/I

Comment: Very preliminary studies might be conducted using exceedingly small samples. While such studies might be useful to the researcher who is testing new methodology, the results frequently are not publishable. Because there are no scientific standards for what constitutes a reasonable sample size for a pilot study to be publishable, consumers of research need to make subjective judgments when answering this evaluation question. Likewise, there are no standards for sample sizes for developmental tests of a theory.

For purposive samples, which are common in qualitative research, the sample size may be determined by the availability of participants who fit the sampling profile for the purposive sample. For instance, to study the career paths of high-achieving women in education, a researcher might decide to use female directors of statewide education agencies. If there are only a handful of such women, the sample will necessarily be limited in number.

On the other hand, when there are many potential participants who meet the standards for a purposive sample, a researcher might continue contacting additional participants until the point of *saturation*, that is, the point at which additional participants are adding little new information to the picture that is emerging from the data the researchers are collecting. In other words, saturation occurs when new participants are revealing the same types of information as those who have already participated. Example 7.3.1 illustrates how this was described in the report of a qualitative study. Note the use of the term *saturation*, which has been italicized for emphasis. Using the criterion of data saturation sometimes results in the use of small samples.

Example 7.3.1[3]

A statement using saturation *to justify the use of a small purposive sample in a qualitative study (italics added for emphasis)*:

Saturation, as described by Lincoln and Guba (1985), was achieved upon interviewing nine dyads, as there was no new or different information emerging; however, a total of 12 dyads were interviewed to confirm redundancy and maintain rigor.

---

[3] Cummings, J. (2011). Sharing a traumatic event: The experience of the listener and the storyteller within the dyad. *Nursing Research*, *60*, 386–392.

Note that those who conduct qualitative research often have extended contact with their participants as a result of using techniques such as in-depth personal interviews or prolonged observational periods. With limited resources, their samples might necessarily be small. On the other hand, quantitative researchers often have more limited contact due to using techniques such as written tests or questionnaires, which can be administered to many participants at little cost. As a result, consumers of research usually should expect quantitative researchers to use larger samples than qualitative researchers.

___ 4. Is the sample size adequate in terms of its orientation (quantitative versus qualitative)?

Very satisfactory 5 4 3 2 1 Very unsatisfactory ***or*** N/A I/I

Comment: Traditionally, quantitative researchers use larger samples than qualitative researchers. For instance, using fewer than 15 participants is quite common and is usually considered acceptable in qualitative research (for reasons, see the discussion under the previous evaluation question). Using such a small number of participants in quantitative research would usually be considered a flaw.[4]

___ 5. If a purposive sample has been used, has the researcher indicated the basis for selecting participants?

Very satisfactory 5 4 3 2 1 Very unsatisfactory ***or*** N/A I/I

Comment: When using purposive sampling, researchers should indicate the basis or criteria for the selection of the participants. Example 7.5.1 is taken from a qualitative study on gender differences in stress among professional managers. Notice that the researchers did not simply rely on managers they happened to know to serve as participants. Instead, they selected a purposive sample of managers that met specific criteria.

Example 7.5.1[5]

A description of the criteria for selecting a purposive sample for a qualitative study:

Participants were selected based on purposive criterion sampling from a list, purchased by the research team, which consisted of professionals who had managerial positions in business, governmental, or nongovernmental organizations in a western Canadian city. The criteria for participation included the following: (a) individuals were responsible for making decisions that affected the direction of their business or organization on a regular basis and (b) individuals

---

[4] Quantitative researchers usually conduct significance tests. Sample size is an important determinant of significance. If the size is very small, a significance test may fail to identify a "true" difference as statistically significant.

[5] Iwasaki, Y., MacKay, K. J., & Ristock, J. (2004). Gender-based analyses of stress among professional managers: An exploratory qualitative study. *International Journal of Stress Management*, *11*, 56–79.

> had to score 3, 4, or 5 on at least three of four questions that asked about level of stress in their work, family, personal life, and overall life situations using a 5-point scale (1 = *not stressful at all* to 5 = *extremely stressful*). The first criterion verified that each individual held a managerial position, whereas the second criterion ensured that the participant generally felt stressed in his or her life. A research assistant randomly called listings from the database to describe the purpose of the study, make sure these individuals met the criteria for being participants, explain the tasks of each participant, and find out whether they were interested in being involved in the study. Attention was also paid to ensuring that both women and men were recruited to participate.

Note that even if a researcher calls his or her sample purposive, usually it should be regarded as merely a sample of convenience unless the specific basis for selection is described.

___ 6. If a population has been studied, has it been clearly identified and described?

Very satisfactory 5 4 3 2 1 Very unsatisfactory ***or*** N/A I/I

Comment: Researchers who conduct population studies often disguise the true identity of their populations (for ethical and legal reasons), especially if the results reflect negatively on the population. Nevertheless, information should be given that helps the reader visualize the population, as illustrated in Example 7.6.1. Notice that the specific city is not mentioned, which helps protect the identity of the participants. Also, note that "prospective interviewees and survey respondents from substance use treatment and child welfare" constitutes the population.

> **Example 7.6.1**[6]
> *Description of a population that was studied*:
>
> First, a purposive sample of prospective interviewees and survey respondents from substance use treatment and child welfare were developed with key contacts at the British Columbia Center for Excellence in Women's Health and the Ministry of Children and Family Development. Prospective interviewees were identified based on the following criteria: (a) experience in working across systems in direct service, consultant, supervisory, or management roles; and (b) representation of different regions in the province. Because a majority of parents who are concurrently involved in child welfare systems are women, special efforts were made to recruit interviewees from agencies whose services include specialized treatment for women with addiction problems. Prospective interviewees were contacted by e-mail to inform them of the purpose of the study and to invite participation. Prospective interviewees who did not respond to ini-

[6] Drabble, L., & Poole, N. (2011). Collaboration between addiction treatment and child welfare fields: Opportunities in a Canadian context. *Journal of Social Work Practice in the Addictions, 11*, 124–149.

> tial contacts received follow-up e-mails and phone calls to invite their participation in the study. Out of 36 prospective interviewees identified for the study, 12 did not respond to preliminary e-mail invitations (66% response rate).

With information such as that provided in Example 7.6.1, readers can make educated judgments as to whether the results are likely to apply to other populations of social workers.

___ **7. Has informed consent been obtained?**

Very satisfactory 5 4 3 2 1 Very unsatisfactory ***or*** N/A I/I

Comment: This evaluation question was raised in the previous chapter on evaluating samples when researchers generalize. (See Evaluation Question 12 in Chapter 6.) It is being raised again in this chapter because it is an important question that applies whether or not researchers are attempting to generalize.

___ **8. Overall, is the description of the sample adequate?**

Very satisfactory 5 4 3 2 1 Very unsatisfactory ***or*** N/A I/I

Comment: Rate this evaluation question after considering your answers to the earlier ones in this chapter and taking into account any additional considerations and concerns you may have.

Exercise for Chapter 7

Part A

Directions: Answer the following questions.

1. Very briefly explain in your own words how theory development might impact the selection of a sample.

2. The use of *purposive* samples is a tradition in which type of research?
   A. Qualitative B. Quantitative

3. Suppose you were evaluating a pilot study on college students' voting behavior. What are some demographics that you think should be described for such a study?

4. Very briefly describe in your own words the meaning of *data saturation*. Is this concept more closely affiliated with quantitative *or* qualitative research?

5. Small samples are more common in which type of research?
   A. Qualitative B. Quantitative

6. Which of the evaluation questions was regarded as so important that it was posed in both Chapter 6 and this chapter?

Part B

Directions: Locate three research reports of interest to you in academic journals in which the researchers are not directly concerned with generalizing from a sample to a population, and apply the evaluation questions in this chapter. Select the one to which you gave the highest overall rating and bring it to class for discussion. Be prepared to discuss its strengths and weaknesses.

Chapter 8

Evaluating Measures

Immediately after describing the sample or population, researchers typically describe their measurement procedures. A *measure* is any tool or method for measuring a trait or characteristic. The description of measures in research reports is usually identified with the subheading *Measures*.[1]

Often, researchers use published measures. About equally as often, researchers use measures that they devise specifically for their particular research purposes. As a general rule, researchers should provide more information about such newly developed measures than on previously published ones that have been described in detail in other publications, such as test manuals and other research reports.

While a consumer of research would need to take several sequential courses in measurement to become an expert, he or she will be able to make preliminary evaluations of researchers' measurement procedures by applying the evaluation questions discussed in this chapter.

___ 1. Have the actual items and questions (or at least a sample of them) been provided?

Very satisfactory 5 4 3 2 1 Very unsatisfactory ***or*** N/A I/I

Comment: Providing sample items and questions is highly desirable because they help to operationalize what was measured. Note that researchers *operationalize* when they specify the physical properties of the concepts on which they are reporting.

In Example 8.1.1, the researchers provide sample items for two areas measured (alcohol and drug use). Note that by being given the actual words used in the questions, consumers of research can evaluate whether the wording is appropriate and unambiguous.

Example 8.1.1[2]

Sample interview questions:

The poly-substance intoxication index asks youth seven questions about their alcohol and drug use (e.g., "Have you ever smoked a cigarette?" "Have you ever

---

[1] As indicated in Chapter 1, *observation* is a broad term that encompasses all forms of measurement. The term *measures* refers to the materials, scales, and tests that are used to make the observations or obtain the measurements. Participants and Measures are typical subheadings under the main heading Method in a research report.

[2] Oelsner, J., Lippold, M. A., & Greenberg, M. T. (2011). Factors influencing the development of school bonding among middle school students. *Journal of Early Adolescence*, *31*, 463–487.

drunk more than just a few sips of alcohol?"), which are answered with 0 (*no*) or 1 (*yes*). The questions ask whether the youth has ever drunk alcohol; smoked cigarettes, marijuana, or hashish; sniffed glue or paint; used ecstasy; used prescription hard drugs or medication; and whether the youth has ever used Vicodin, Percocet, or Oxycontin. The index ranges from 0 to 7, with 7 indicating the use of all substances.

Example 8.1.2 also illustrates this guideline. The questions were asked in a qualitative study in which the questions were open-ended.

Example 8.1.2[3]

Questions used in a qualitative study:

Respondents were asked, via an anonymous online survey, to provide comments about the former colleague's strengths and weaknesses as a leader. For the comment focusing on strengths, the instructions read, "We'd like to hear your views about this person's strengths as a colleague and as a leader. Please write a few brief thoughts below." For the comment focusing on weaknesses, the instructions read, "Consider areas where you think this person could improve as a colleague and leader. What do you wish they would do differently...what do you wish they would change? Please be honest and constructive." To minimize contrived or meaningless responses, we informed raters that the comments were optional: "These comments are important, but if nothing constructive comes to mind, click below to continue."

Many achievement tests have items that vary in difficulty. When this is the case, including sample items that show the range of difficulty is desirable. The researchers who wrote Example 8.1.3 did this.

Example 8.1.3[4]

Sample achievement items that show their range of difficulty:

This task [mental computation of word problems] was taken from the arithmetic subtest of the WISC-III (Wechsler, 1991). Each word problem was orally presented and was solved without paper or pencil. Questions ranged from simple addition (e.g., If I cut an apple in half, how many pieces will I have?) to more complex calculations (e.g., If three children buy tickets to the show for $6.00 each, how much change do they get back from $20.00?).

Keep in mind that many measures are copyrighted, and their copyright holders might insist on keeping the actual items secure from public exposure. Obviously, a researcher should not be faulted for failing to provide samples when this is the case.

---

[3] Ames, D. R., & Flynn, F. J. (2007). What breaks a leader: The curvilinear relation between assertiveness and leadership. *Journal of Personality and Social Psychology*, *92*, 307–324.

[4] Swanson, H. L., & Beebe-Frankenberger, M. (2004). The relationship between working memory and mathematical problem solving in children at risk and not at risk for serious math difficulties. *Journal of Educational Psychology*, *96*, 471–491.

___ 2. Are any specialized response formats, settings, and/or restrictions described in detail?

Very satisfactory 5 4 3 2 1 Very unsatisfactory ***or*** N/A I/I

Comment: It is desirable for researchers to indicate the response format (e.g., multiple-choice, responses on a scale from Strongly Agree to Strongly Disagree, and so on).

Examples of settings that should be mentioned are the place where the measures were used (such as in the participants' homes) and whether other individuals were present (such as whether parents were present while their children were interviewed).

Examples of restrictions that should be mentioned are time limits and tools that participants are permitted (or are not permitted) to use, such as not allowing the use of calculators during a mathematics test.

Qualitative researchers also should provide details on these matters. This is illustrated in Example 8.2.1, in which the person who conducted the qualitative interviews is indicated as well as the length of the interviews, the languages used, and the incentive to participate.

Example 8.2.1[5]

Description of data collection in a qualitative study:

After informed consent was obtained, the first author interviewed adolescents twice and nonparental adults once. Each interview lasted 30–90 minutes and was conducted in English or Spanish, as per participants' choice. Participants were paid $10 per interview session. Interviews were audiotaped and transcribed verbatim. Transcripts were verified against audiotapes by the research team. All names were removed from the transcripts to ensure confidentiality.

___ 3. When appropriate, were multiple methods used to collect data/information on each variable?

Very satisfactory 5 4 3 2 1 Very unsatisfactory ***or*** N/A I/I

Comment: As indicated in Chapter 1, it is safe to assume that all methods of observation (e.g., testing, interviewing, making observations) are flawed. Thus, the results of a study can be more definitive if more than one method for collecting data is used for each variable.

In quantitative research, researchers emphasize the development of objective measures that meet statistical standards for reliability and validity, which are discussed later in this chapter. When researchers use these highly developed measures, they often do not believe that it is important to use multiple measures. For instance, they might use a well-established multiple-choice reading comprehension test that was ex-

---

[5] Sanchez, B., Reyes, O., & Singh, J. (2006). A qualitative examination of the relationships that serve a mentoring function for Mexican American older adolescents. *Cultural Diversity and Ethnic Minority Psychology*, *12*, 615–631.

tensively investigated (with regard to its validity and reliability) prior to publication of the test. A quantitative researcher would be *unlikely* to supplement such highly developed measures with other measures such as teachers' ratings of students' reading comprehension or some other measurement technique such as having each child read aloud and discuss what they learned from reading. Thus, it is not traditional to use multiple measures of each variable in quantitative research.

In qualitative research, researchers are more likely to use multiple measures of a single phenomenon for several reasons.[6] First, qualitative researchers strive to conduct research that is intensive and yields highly detailed results (often in the form of themes supported by verbal descriptions—as opposed to numbers). The use of multiple measures helps qualitative researchers probe more intensively from different points of view. In addition, qualitative researchers tend to view their research as exploratory. In advance of conducting exploratory research, it is difficult to know which type of measure for a particular variable is likely to be most useful. Finally, qualitative researchers see the use of multiple measures as a way to check the validity of their results. In other words, if different measures of the same phenomenon yield highly consistent results, the validity of the measures (including the interpretation of the data) might be more highly regarded as being valid than if only one data source was used.

Sometimes, it is not realistic to expect researchers to use multiple measures of all variables. For instance, measurement of some variables is so straightforward that it would be a poor use of a researcher's time to measure them in several ways. For example, most researchers would be very confident in the validity of asking second-grade students to perform the one-digit multiplication facts on a paper-and-pencil test. It would be needlessly redundant to ask the students to demonstrate their achievement a second time by having an interviewer ask the same students to answer the same multiplication facts.

___ 4. For published measures, have sources been cited where additional information can be obtained?

Very satisfactory 5 4 3 2 1 Very unsatisfactory ***or*** N/A I/I

Comment: Researchers should provide references to sources of additional information on the published measures used in their research.

Some measures are "published" only in the sense that they were previously reproduced in full in journal articles. Such articles typically describe the development and statistical properties of the measures. Other measures are published by commercial publishers as separate publications (e.g., test booklets) that usually have accompanying manuals that describe technical information on the measures.

In Example 8.4.1, the researchers briefly describe the nature of one of the measures they used, following it with a statement that the validity and reliability of the

---

[6] Qualitative researchers often use the term *triangulation of data sources* when they use multiple measures for the same purpose.

measure have been established. It is important to note that they provide a reference (i.e., Maclean & Lecci, 2000; Stewart, Loughlin, & Rhyno, 2001) where more information on the measure's reliability and validity may be found.

Example 8.4.1[7]

Brief description of a measure in which a reference for more information on reliability and validity is provided (bold added for emphasis):

Motivations for drinking alcohol were assessed using the 20-item Drinking Motives Questionnaire (DMQ-R; Cooper, 1994), encompassing the 4 subscales of Coping (α = .87), Conformity (α = .79), Enhancement (α = .92), and Social Motives (α = .94). **The DMQ-R has proven to be the most rigorously tested and validated measurement of drinking motives (Maclean & Lecci, 2000; Stewart, Loughlin, & Rhyno, 2001).** Respondents were prompted with, "Thinking of the time you drank in the past 30 days, how often would you say that you drank for the following reasons?" Participants rated each reason (e.g., "because it makes social gatherings more fun" and "to fit in") on a 1 (*almost never/never*) to 5 (*almost always/always*).

In Example 8.4.2, the researchers also briefly describe the nature of one of the measures they used, following it with a statement that describes its technical and statistical properties, including reliability and validity.

Example 8.4.2[8]

Brief description of a measure in which a reference for more information is provided (bold added for emphasis):

Youths completed the RSE (Rosenberg, 1979), a 10-item scale assessing the degree to which respondents are satisfied with their lives and feel good about themselves. Children respond on a 4-point scale, ranging from 1 (*strongly agree*) to 4 (*strongly disagree*); higher scores indicate more positive self-esteem. **Studies across a wide range of ages yield adequate internal consistency (α between .77 to .88), temporal stability (test-retest correlations between .82 and .88), and construct validity (i.e., moderate correlations with other measures of self-concept and depression symptoms) (Blascovich & Tomeka, 1993).**

[7] LaBrie, J. W., Kenney, S. R., Migliuri, S., & Lac, A. (2011). Sexual experience and risky alcohol consumption among incoming first-year college females. *Journal of Child & Adolescents Substance Abuse, 20*, 15–33.

[8] Goodman, S. H., Tully, E., Connell, A. M., Hartman, C. L., & Huh, M. (2011). Measuring children's perceptions of their mother's depression: The Children's Perceptions of Others' Depression Scale–Mother Version. *Journal of Family Psychology, 25*, 163–173.

___ 5. When delving into sensitive matters, is there reason to believe that accurate data were obtained?

Very satisfactory 5 4 3 2 1 Very unsatisfactory *or* N/A I/I

Comment: Some issues are sensitive because they deal with illegal matters such as illicit substance use, gang violence, and so on. Others are sensitive because of societal taboos such as those regarding certain forms of sexual behavior. Still others may be sensitive because of idiosyncratic personal views on privacy. For instance, age and income are sensitive issues for many individuals. Participants often decline to answer these questions or may not answer honestly. Thus, self-reports by participants may sometimes lack validity. The authors of Example 8.5.1 discuss the limitations of self-reports and how they might have affected the results of their research.

Example 8.5.1[9]

Discussion of limitations of self-reports in relation to a particular study:

Our data are based exclusively on self-reported assessments of psychological distress, and, thus, our ability to draw conclusions is limited by the validity and reliability of this methodology. In general, self-report data are subject to threats to validity such as social desirability and response-style biases.[10] Thus, as suggested above, it may be that the veterans in the treatment groups were hesitant to acknowledge much change in the status of their distress as they may fear that to do so would impact their service connection or their identity associated with being a traumatized veteran.

A common technique for encouraging honest answers to sensitive questions is to collect the responses anonymously. For instance, participants may be asked to mail in questionnaires with the assurance that they are not coded in any way that would reveal their identity. In group settings, participants who respond in writing may also be assured that their responses are anonymous. However, if a group is small, such as a class of 20 students, some participants might be hesitant to be perfectly honest regarding highly sensitive matters because a small group does not provide much "cover" for hiding the identity of a participant who engages in illegal or taboo behaviors.

With techniques such as interviewing or direct physical observation, it is usually not possible to provide anonymity. The most a researcher might be able to do is assure *confidentiality*. Such an assurance is likely to work best if the participants already know and trust the interviewer (such as a school counselor) or if the researcher has spent enough time with the participants to develop rapport and trust. The latter is more likely to occur in qualitative research than quantitative research because qualitative re-

---

[9] Bolton, E. E. et al. (2004). Evaluating a cognitive–behavioral group treatment program for veterans with posttraumatic stress disorder. *Psychological Services*, *1*, 140–146.

[10] *Social desirability* refers to the tendency of some respondents to provide answers citing behaviors that are considered socially desirable. *Response-style bias* refers to the tendency of some respondents to respond in certain ways (such as tending to select the middle category on a scale) regardless of the content of the question.

searchers often spend substantial amounts of time interacting with their participants in an effort to bond with them.

___ 6. Have steps been taken to keep the measures from influencing any overt behaviors that were observed?

Very satisfactory 5 4 3 2 1 Very unsatisfactory ***or*** N/A I/I

Comment: If participants know they are being directly observed, they may temporarily change their behavior. Clearly, this is likely to happen in the study of highly sensitive behaviors, but it can also affect data collection on other matters. For instance, some students may show their best behavior if they come to class to find a newly installed video camera scanning the classroom (to gather research data). Other students may show off by acting up in the presence of the camera.

One solution would be to make surreptitious observations, such as with a hidden video camera or a one-way mirror. In most circumstances, such techniques raise serious ethical and legal problems.

Another solution is to make the observational procedures a routine part of the research setting. For instance, if it is routine for a classroom to be visited frequently by outsiders (e.g., parents, school staff, and university observers), the presence of a researcher may be unlikely to obtrude on the behavior of the students.

___ 7. If the collection and coding of observations involves subjectivity, is there evidence of interobserver reliability?

Very satisfactory 5 4 3 2 1 Very unsatisfactory ***or*** N/A I/I

Comment: Suppose a researcher observes groups of adolescent females interacting in various public settings, such as shopping malls, in order to collect data on aggressive behavior. Identifying some aggressive behaviors may require considerable subjectivity. If an adolescent puffs out her chest, is this a threatening behavior or merely a manifestation of a big sigh of relief? Is a scowl a sign of aggression or merely an expression of unhappiness? Answering such questions sometimes requires considerable subjectivity.

An important technique for addressing this issue is to have two or more independent observers make observations of the same participants at the same time. If the *rate of agreement* on the identification and classification of the behavior is reasonably high (say, 80% or more), a consumer of research will be assured that the resulting data are not idiosyncratic to one particular observer and his or her powers of observation and possible biases.

In Example 8.7.1, the researchers reported rates of agreement of 90% and 96%. Note that to achieve such high rates of agreement the researchers first trained the raters by instructing them to rate the behavior with groups that were not part of the main study.

Example 8.7.1[11]

Discussion of limitations of self-reports in relation to a particular study:

Two independent raters first practiced the categorization of self-disclosure on five group sessions that were not part of this study and discussed each category until full agreement was reached. Next, each rater identified the "predominant behavior" (Hill & O'Brien, 1999)—that is, the speech turn that contained the disclosure—on which they reached agreement on 90%. Finally, each rater classified the participants into the three levels of self-disclosure. Interrater agreement was high (96%).

The rate of agreement often is referred to as *interobserver reliability*. When the observations are reduced to scores for each participant (such as a total score for nonverbal aggressiveness), the scores based on two independent observers' observations can be expressed as an *interobserver reliability coefficient*. In reliability studies, these can range from 0.00 to 1.00, with coefficients of about 0.70 or higher indicating adequate interobserver reliability.[12]

___ 8. If a measure is designed to measure a single unitary trait, does it have adequate internal consistency?

Very satisfactory 5 4 3 2 1 Very unsatisfactory ***or*** N/A I/I

Comment: A test of computational skills in mathematics at the primary grade levels measures a relatively homogeneous trait. However, a mathematics battery that measures verbal problem solving and mathematical reasoning in addition to computational skills measures a more heterogeneous trait. Likewise, a self-report measure of depression measures a much more homogeneous trait than does a measure of overall mental health.

For measures designed to measure homogeneous traits, it is important to ask whether they are *internally consistent* (i.e., to what extent do the items within the measure yield results that are consistent with each other?). While it is beyond the scope of this book to explain how and why it works, a statistic known as Cronbach's alpha (whose symbol is α) provides a statistical measure of internal consistency.[13] As a special type of correlation coefficient, it ranges from 0.00 to 1.00, with values of about 0.70 or above indicating adequate internal consistency and values above 0.90 indicating excellence on this characteristic. Values below 0.70 suggest that more than

[11] Shechtman, Z., & Rybko, J. (2004). Attachment style and observed initial self-disclosure as explanatory variables of group functioning. *Group Dynamics: Theory, Research, and Practice*, *8*, 207–220.

[12] Mathematically, these coefficients are the same as *correlation coefficients*, which are covered in all standard introductory statistics courses. Correlation coefficients can range from –1.00 to 1.00, with a value of 0.00 indicating no relationship. In practice, however, negatives are not found in reliability studies. Values near 1.00 indicate a high rate of agreement.

[13] *Split-half reliability* also measures internal consistency, but Cronbach's alpha is widely considered a superior measure. Hence, split-half reliability is seldom reported.

one trait is being measured by the measure, which is undesirable when a researcher wants to measure only one homogeneous trait.

In Example 8.8.1, the values of Cronbach's alpha are above the cutoff point of 0.70.

Example 8.8.1[14]

Statement regarding internal consistency using Cronbach's alpha:

The 90-item Unisex Edition of the American College Testing Interest Inventory (UNIACT; Lamb & Prediger, 1981) was used for assessment of six interest themes identified by Holland (1973): Realistic (α = .86), Investigative (α = .92), Artistic (α = .91), Social (α = .83), Enterprising (α = .88), and Conventional (α = .92); source for Cronbach's alpha is Ackerman et al. (2001). The items (15 per scale) assess an individual's preference for specific job tasks.

Internal consistency usually is regarded as an issue only when a measure is designed to measure a single homogeneous trait *and* when the measure yields scores (as opposed to measures such as interviews when they are used to identify patterns that are described in words). If a measure does not meet these two criteria, "not applicable" is an appropriate answer to this evaluation question.

___ 9. For stable traits, is there evidence of temporal stability?

Very satisfactory 5 4 3 2 1 Very unsatisfactory ***or*** N/A I/I

Comment: Suppose a researcher wants to measure aptitude (i.e., potential) for learning algebra. Such an aptitude is widely regarded as being stable. In other words, it is unlikely to fluctuate much from one week to another. Hence, a test of such an aptitude should yield results that are stable across at least short periods of time. For instance, if a student's score on such a test administered this week indicates that he or she has very little aptitude for learning algebra, this test should yield a similar assessment if administered to the same student next week.

Likewise, in the area of personality measurement, most measures also should yield results that have temporal stability (i.e., are stable over time). For instance, a researcher would expect that a student who scored very highly on a measure of self-esteem one week would also score very highly the following week because self-esteem is unlikely to fluctuate much over short periods of time.

The most straightforward approach to assessing temporal stability (e.g., stability of the measurements over time) is to administer a measure to a group of participants twice at different points in time—typically with a couple of weeks between administrations. The two sets of scores can be correlated, and if a coefficient (whose symbol is r) of about 0.70 or more (on a scale from 0.00 to 1.00) is obtained, there is evidence of temporal stability. This type of reliability is commonly known as *test-retest reliabil-*

---

[14] Ackerman, P. L., & Beier, M. E. (2006). Determinants of domain knowledge and independent study learning in an adult sample. *Journal of Educational Psychology*, *98*, 366–381.

ity. It is usually examined only for tests or scales that yield scores (as opposed to open-ended interviews, which yield words as responses).

In Example 8.9.1, researchers describe how they established the test-retest reliability of a measure. Note that they use the symbol *r* and report values well above the suggested cutoff point of 0.70.

Example 8.9.1[15]
Statement regarding temporal stability (test-retest reliability) established by the researchers:

In order to assess the test-retest reliability, the G-ECR-R was administered to a separate sample of undergraduate students ($N = 51$) twice over a 3-week period. The test-retest reliability was $r = .85$...for the avoidance subscale and $r = .88$ for the anxiety subscale....

In Example 8.9.2, the researchers report on the range of test-retest reliability coefficients that were reported earlier by other researchers (i.e., McNeilly et al., 1996). All of them were above the suggested 0.70 cutoff point for acceptability.

Example 8.9.2[16]
Statement regarding temporal stability (test-retest reliability):

The PRS [Perceived Racism Scale] is a 32-item instrument that measures emotional reactions to racism [in four domains].... McNeilly et al. (1996) reported...test-retest reliability coefficients ranging from .71 to .80 for the four domains.

___ 10. When appropriate, is there evidence of content validity?

Very satisfactory 5 4 3 2 1 Very unsatisfactory ***or*** N/A I/I

Comment: An important issue in the evaluation of achievement tests is the extent to which the contents of the tests (i.e., the stimulus materials and skills) are suitable in light of the research purpose. For instance, if a researcher has used an achievement test to study the extent to which the second graders in a school district have achieved the skills expected of them at this grade level, a consumer of the research will want to know whether the contents of the test are aligned with (or match) the contents of the second-grade curriculum.

While content validity is most closely associated with measurement of achievement, it also is sometimes used as a construct for evaluating other types of measures.

---

[15] Tsagarakis, M., Kafetsios, K., & Stalikas, A. (2007). Reliability and validity of the Greek version of the Revised Experiences in Close Relationships measure of adult attachment. *European Journal of Psychological Assessment*, *23*, 47–55.

[16] Liang, C. T. H., Li, L. C., & Kim, B. S. K. (2004). The Asian American Racism-Related Stress Inventory: Development, factor analysis, reliability, and validity. *Journal of Counseling Psychology*, *51*, 103–114.

For instance, in Example 8.10.1, the researchers had the contents of the measure evaluated by experts.

Example 8.10.1[17]

A measure subjected to content validation:

To test content validity, the C-PDSS [Chinese Version of the Postpartum Depression Screening Scale] was submitted to a panel consisting of six experts from different fields, including a psychology professor, a clinician from a psychiatric clinic, a senior nurse in psychiatric and mental health nursing, a university professor in obstetric nursing, and two obstetricians from two regional public hospitals.... The rating of each item was based on two criteria: (a) the applicability of the content (applicability of expression and content to the local culture and the research object) and (b) the clarity of phrasing.

___ 11. When appropriate, is there evidence of empirical validity?

Very satisfactory 5 4 3 2 1 Very unsatisfactory ***or*** N/A I/I

Comment: Empirical validity refers to validity established by collecting data using a measure in order to determine the extent to which the data make sense. For instance, a depression scale might be empirically validated by being administered to an institutionalized, clinically depressed group of adult patients as well as to a random sample of adult patients visiting family physicians for annual checkups. A researcher would expect the scores of the two groups to differ substantially in a predicted direction (i.e., the institutionalized sample should have higher depression scores). If they do not, the validity of the scale would be questionable.

Sometimes, the empirical validity of a test is expressed with a correlation coefficient. For instance, a test maker might correlate scores on the College Board's SATs with freshman grades in college. A correlation of .40 or more might be interpreted as indicating that the test has validity as a modest predictor of college grades.

Empirical validity comes in many forms, and a full exploration of it is beyond the scope of this book. Some key terms that suggest that empirical validity has been explored are *predictive validity*, *concurrent validity*, *criterion-related validity*, *convergent validity*, *discriminate validity*, *construct validity*, and *factor analysis*.

When researchers describe empirical validity, they usually briefly summarize the information, and these summaries are typically fairly comprehensible to individuals with limited training in tests and measurements.

In Example 8.11.1, the researchers briefly describe the empirical validity of a measure they used in their research. Notice that sources where additional information may be obtained are cited.

---

[17] Li, L., Liu, F., Zhang, H., Wang, L., & Chen, X. (2011). Chinese version of the Postpartum Depression Screening Scale: Translation and validation. *Nursing Research, 60*, 231–239.

Example 8.11.1[18]

Statement regarding empirical validity of a measure with a reference to sources where more information may be obtained:

Supporting the convergent validity of the measure, PGIS [Personal Growth Initiative Scale] scores correlated positively with assertiveness, internal locus of control, and instrumentality among both European American (Robitschek, 1998) and Mexican American college students (Robitschek, 2003).

Often, information on validity is exceptionally brief. For instance, in Example 8.11.2, the researchers refer to the validity of a questionnaire as "excellent." The source that is cited (McDowell & Newell, 1996) would need to be consulted to determine whether this refers to empirical validity.

Example 8.11.2[19]

Statement regarding empirical validity of a measure with a reference to where more information may be obtained:

We assessed general psychological distress using the 12-item version of the General Health Questionnaire (GHQ-12; Goldberg & Huxley, 1992; McDowell & Newell, 1996). This scale, based on a 4-point Likert scale, was designed to be a broad screening instrument for psychological problems in a general population and has excellent validity and reliability (McDowell & Newell, 1996).

Note that it is traditional for researchers to address empirical validity only for measures that yield scores, as opposed to measures such as semi-structured, open-ended interviews.

___ 12. Do the researchers discuss obvious limitations of their measures?

Very satisfactory 5 4 3 2 1 Very unsatisfactory ***or*** N/A I/I

Comment: By discussing limitations of their measures, researchers help consumers of research to understand the extent to which the data presented in the results can be trusted. In Example 8.5.1, the researchers discussed how the limitations of using self-reports might have affected the outcomes of their study. In Example 8.12.1, the researchers discuss other possible limitations.

[18] Hardin, E. E., Weigold, I. K., Robitschek, C., & Nixon, A. E. (2007). Self-discrepancy and distress: The role of a personal growth initiative. *Journal of Counseling Psychology*, *54*, 86–92.

[19] Adams, R. E., Boscarino, J. A., & Figley, C. R. (2006). Compassion fatigue and psychological distress among social workers: A validation study. *American Journal of Orthopsychiatry*, *76*, 103–108.

Example 8.12.1[20]
Statement acknowledging a weakness in measures:

With regard to measurement, it should be noted that the history of victimization measure was limited by a one-year historical time frame. This time frame might have excluded youths who were still experiencing the traumatic effects of victimizing events that occurred over a year before their completion of the survey. The victimization measure was also limited in that it did not include a measure of sexual victimization for male youths.

If, in your judgment, there are no obvious limitations to the measures described in a research report, a rating of N/A (not applicable) should be made for this evaluation question.

___ 13. Overall, are the measures adequate?

Very satisfactory 5 4 3 2 1 Very unsatisfactory ***or*** N/A I/I

Comment: The amount of information about measures used in research that is reported in academic journals is often quite limited. The provision of references for obtaining additional information helps to overcome this problem.

Typically, if a researcher provides too little information for a consumer of research to make an informed judgment and/or does not provide references where additional information can be obtained, the consumer should give it a low rating on this evaluation question or respond that there is insufficient information (I/I).

Exercise for Chapter 8

Part A

Directions: Answer the following questions.

1. Name two or three issues that some participants might regard as sensitive and, hence, are difficult to measure. Answer this question with examples that are *not* mentioned in this chapter. (See the discussion of Evaluation Question 5.)

2. Have you ever changed your behavior because you knew (or thought) you were being observed? If yes, briefly describe how or why you were being observed and what behavior(s) you changed. (See Evaluation Question 6.)

---

[20] Williams, K. A., & Chapman, M. V. (2011). Comparing health and mental health needs, service use, and barriers to services among sexual minority youths and their peers. *Health & Social Work*, *36*, 197–206.

3. According to this chapter, what is a reasonably high rate of agreement when two or more independent observers classify behavior (i.e., of interobserver reliability)?

4. For which of the following would it be more important to consider internal consistency using Cronbach's alpha? Explain your answer.
   A. For a single test of mathematics ability for first graders that yields a single score.
   B. For a single test of reading and mathematics abilities for first graders that yields a single score.

5. Suppose a researcher obtained a test-retest reliability coefficient of 0.86. According to this chapter, does this indicate adequate temporal stability? Explain.

6. Which type of validity is mentioned in this chapter as being an especially important issue in the evaluation of achievement tests?

Part B

Directions: Locate two research reports of interest to you in academic journals. Evaluate the descriptions of the measures in light of the evaluation questions in this chapter, taking into account any other considerations and concerns you may have. Select the one to which you gave the highest overall rating, and bring it to class for discussion. Be prepared to discuss both its strengths and weaknesses.

Chapter 9

Evaluating Experimental Procedures

An experiment is a study in which treatments are given in order to determine their effects. For instance, one group of students might be trained to use conflict-resolution techniques (the experimental group) while a control group is not given any training. Then, the students in both groups could be observed on the playground to determine whether the experimental group uses more conflict-resolution techniques than the control group.

The treatments (i.e., training versus no training) constitute what are known as the *independent variables*, which are sometimes called the *stimuli* or *input variables*. The resulting behavior on the playground constitutes the *dependent variable*, which is sometimes called the *output* or *response variable*.

Any study in which even a single treatment is given to just a single participant is an experiment as long as the purpose of the study is to determine the effects of the treatment on another variable. A study that does not meet this minimal condition is *not* an experiment. Thus, for instance, a political poll in which questions are asked but no treatments are given is *not* an experiment and should *not* be referred to as such.

The following evaluation questions cover basic guidelines for the evaluation of experiments.

___ 1. If two or more groups were compared, were the participants assigned at random to the groups?

Very satisfactory 5 4 3 2 1 Very unsatisfactory ***or*** N/A I/I

Comment: Assigning participants at random to groups guarantees that there is no bias in the assignment. For instance, random assignment to two groups in the experiment on conflict-resolution training (mentioned previously) would provide assurance that there is no bias, such as systematically assigning the less-aggressive children to the experimental group.

Note that it is *not* safe to assume the assignment was random unless a researcher explicitly states that it was. Example 9.1.1 illustrates how this was stated in reports on three different experiments.

Example 9.1.1

Excerpts from three experiments with random assignment explicitly mentioned:

Experiment 1: Participants ages 14 to 18 years were randomly assigned to each flicker-type condition.[1]

Experiment 2: Using an experimental design, 150 college football players were randomly assigned to four conditions in which they read different vignettes about Jack, a football player who cries after a football game.[2]

Experiment 3: Socially anxious students were randomly assigned to either the experimental group, which received video and social feedback (n = 12), or the control group (n = 13).[3]

Note that assigning *individuals* to treatments at random is vastly superior to assigning previously existing *groups* to treatments at random. For instance, in educational research, it is not uncommon to assign one class to an experimental treatment and have another class serve as the control group. Because students are not ordinarily randomly assigned to classes, there may be systematic differences between the students in the two classes. For instance, one class might have more highly motivated students, another might have more parental involvement, and so on. Thus, a consumer of research should *not* answer "yes" to this evaluation question unless *individuals* were assigned at random.

If the answer to this evaluation question is "yes," the experiment being evaluated is known as a *true experiment*. Note that this term does not imply that the experiment is perfect in all respects. Instead, it indicates only that participants were assigned at random to comparison groups.

___ **2. If two or more comparison groups were not formed at random, is there evidence that they were initially equal in important ways?**

Very satisfactory 5 4 3 2 1 Very unsatisfactory ***or*** N/A I/I

Comment: Suppose a researcher wants to study the impact of a new third grade reading program being used with all third graders in a school (the experimental group). For a control group, the researcher will have to use third graders in another school.[4] Because students are not randomly assigned to schools, this experiment will get low

[1] Huang, K.-C., Lin, R.-T., & Wu, C.-F. (2011). Effects of flicker rate, complexity, and color combinations of Chinese characters and backgrounds on visual search performance with varying flicker types. *Perceptual and Motor Skills*, *113*, 201–214.

[2] Wong, Y. J., Steinfeldt, J. A., LaFollettte, J. R., & Tsao, S.-C. (2011). Men's tears: Football players' evaluations of crying behavior. *Psychology of Men & Masculinity*, *12*, 297–310.

[3] Kanai, Y., Sasagawa, S., Chen, J., & Sakano, Y. (2011). The effects of video and nonnegative social feedback on distorted appraisals of bodily sensations and social anxiety. *Psychological Reports*, *109*, 411–427.

[4] The use of two intact groups (groups that were already formed) with both a pretest and a posttest is known as a *quasi-experiment*—as opposed to a *true experiment*.

marks on Evaluation Question 1. However, if the researcher selects a control school in which the first graders have standardized reading test scores similar to those in the experimental school and are similar in other important respects such as parents' socioeconomic status, the experiment may yield useful experimental evidence.

Note, however, that similarity between groups is not as satisfactory as assigning participants at random to groups. For instance, the children in the two schools in the example being considered may be different in some important respect that the researcher has overlooked or on which the researcher has no information. Perhaps the children's teachers in the experimental school are more experienced. Their experience in teaching, rather than the new reading program, might be the cause of any differences in reading achievement between the two groups.

When using two intact groups (such as classrooms), it is important to give both a pretest and a posttest to measure the dependent variable. For instance, to evaluate the reading program, a researcher should give a pretest in reading, in order to establish whether the two intact groups are initially similar on the dependent variable. Of course, if the two groups are highly dissimilar, the results of the experiment will be difficult to interpret.[5]

___ 3. If only a single participant or a single group is used, have the treatments been alternated?

Very satisfactory 5 4 3 2 1 Very unsatisfactory ***or*** N/A I/I

Comment: Not all experiments involve the comparison of two or more groups. Consider, for instance, a teacher who wants to try using increased praise for appropriate behaviors in the classroom to see if it reduces behaviors such as inappropriate out-of-seat behavior (IOSB). To conduct an experiment on this, the teacher could count the number of IOSBs for a week or two before administering the increased praise. This would yield what is called the *baseline data*. Suppose the teacher then introduces the extra praise and finds a decrease in the IOSBs. This might suggest that the extra praise *caused* the improvement. However, such a conclusion would be highly tenuous because children's environments are constantly changing in many ways, and some other environmental influence (such as the school principal scolding the students on the playground without the teacher's knowledge) might be the real cause of the change. A more definitive test would be for the teacher to reverse the treatment and go back to giving less praise, then revert to the higher-praise condition. If the data form the expected pattern, the teacher would have reasonable evidence that increased praise reduces IOSB.

[5] If the groups are initially dissimilar, a researcher should consider locating another group that is more similar to serve as the control. If this is not possible, a statistical technique known as analysis of covariance can be used to adjust the posttest scores in light of the initial differences in pretest scores. Such a statistical adjustment can be risky if the assumptions underlying the test have been violated, a topic beyond the scope of this book.

Notice that in the example being considered, the single group serves as the control group during the baseline, serves as the experimental group when the extra praise is initially given, serves as the control group again when the condition is reversed, and finally serves as the experimental group again when the extra praise is reintroduced. Such a design has this strength: The same children with the same backgrounds are both the experimental and control groups. (In a two-group experiment, the children in one group may be different from the children in the other group in some important way that affects the outcome of the experiment.) The major drawback of a single-group design is that the same children are being exposed to multiple treatments, which may lead to unnatural reactions. How does a child feel when some weeks he or she gets extra praise for appropriate behaviors but other weeks does not? Such reactions might confound the results of the experiment.[6]

If two classes were available for the type of experiment being considered, a teacher could use what is called a *multiple baseline design*, in which the initial extra-praise condition is started on a different week for each group. If the pattern of decreased IOSB under the extra-praise condition holds up across both groups, the causal conclusion would be even stronger than when only one group was used at one point in time.

The type of experimentation being discussed under this evaluation question is often referred to as *single-subject research* or *behavior analysis*. When a researcher has only a single participant or one intact group that cannot be divided at random into two or more groups, such a design can provide useful information about causality.

___ 4. Are the treatments described in sufficient detail?

Very satisfactory 5 4 3 2 1 Very unsatisfactory ***or*** N/A I/I

Comment: Because the purpose of an experiment is to estimate the effects of the treatments on dependent variables, researchers should provide detailed descriptions of the treatments that were administered. If the treatments are complex, such as two types of therapy in clinical psychology, researchers should provide references to additional publications where detailed accounts can be found, if possible.

In Example 9.4.1, the researchers begin by giving references for the experimental task, and then they describe how it was used in their study. Only a portion of their detailed description of the treatment is shown in the example.

Example 9.4.1[7]

Excerpt showing references for more information on experimental treatment followed by a detailed description (partial description shown here):

The 6.3 min video was titled *Bullying or Not?* (available online at

[6] Researchers refer to this problem as *multiple-treatment interference*.

[7] Baly, M. W., & Cornell, D. G. (2011). Effects of an educational video on the measurement of bullying by self-report. *Journal of School Violence, 10*, 221–238.

www.youtube.com) because it was designed to help students distinguish bullying from other forms of peer conflict. In the opening scene of the video, two student commentators (boy and girl) reviewed the definition of bullying, emphasizing the power imbalance concept. Next, three pairs of scenes illustrated the difference between bullying and ordinary peer conflict that is not bullying. In each pair, the first scene demonstrated a clear instance of bullying, and in the companion scene, the same actors enacted a similar peer conflict that was not bullying. For example, two scenes illustrated the difference between verbal bullying and a verbal argument between two peers of comparable size and status. Similarly, two scenes distinguished social bullying from an argument between friends, and two scenes distinguished physical bullying from a physical struggle between two boys of comparable size and strength. The student commentators explained the power imbalance present in each of the bullying scenes. At the end of the video, the student commentators emphasized the importance of preventing bullying and encouraged students to answer survey questions correctly when asked about bullying.

___ 5. If the treatments were administered by individuals other than the researcher, were those individuals properly trained?

Very satisfactory 5 4 3 2 1 Very unsatisfactory ***or*** N/A I/I

Comment: Researchers often rely on other individuals, such as graduate assistants, teachers, and psychologists, to administer the treatments they use in experiments. When this is the case, it is desirable for the researcher to assure consumers of research that there was proper training. Otherwise, it is possible that the treatments were modified in some unknown way. Example 9.5.1 shows a statement regarding the training of student therapists who administered treatments in an experiment. Note that such statements are typically brief.

Example 9.5.1[8]

Excerpt on training those who administered the treatments:

Student therapists received 54 hr of training in EFT–AS [emotion-focused therapy for adult survivors of child abuse]. This consisted of reviewing the treatment manual and videotapes of therapy sessions with expert therapists, as well as supervised peer skills practice and three sessions of therapy with volunteer "practice" clients.

---

[8] Paivio, S. C., Holowaty, K. A. M., & Hall, I. E. (2004). The influence of therapist adherence and competence on client reprocessing of child abuse memories. *Psychotherapy: Theory, Research, Practice, Training, 41*, 56–68.

___ 6. If the treatments were administered by individuals other than the researcher, were they monitored?

Very satisfactory 5 4 3 2 1 Very unsatisfactory ***or*** N/A I/I

Comment: Even if those who administered the treatments were trained, they normally should be monitored. This is especially true for long and complex treatment cycles. For instance, if psychologists will be trying out new techniques with clients over a period of several months, the psychologists should be monitored by spot-checking their efforts to determine whether they are applying the techniques they learned in their training. This can be done by directly observing them or by questioning them.

___ 7. If each treatment group had a different person administering a treatment, did the researcher try to eliminate the personal effect?

Very satisfactory 5 4 3 2 1 Very unsatisfactory ***or*** N/A I/I

Comment: Suppose that the purpose of an experiment is to compare the effectiveness of three methods for teaching decoding skills in first-grade reading instruction. If each method is used by a different teacher, differences in the teachers (such as ability to build rapport with students, level of enthusiasm, ability to build effective relationships with parents) may cause any observed differences in achievement (i.e., they may have had a personal effect on the outcome).

One solution to this problem is to have each of the three methods used by a large number of teachers, with the teachers assigned at random to the methods. If such a large-scale study is not possible, another solution is to have each teacher use all three methods. In other words, Teacher A could use Method X, Method Y, and Method Z at different points in time with different children. The other two teachers would do likewise. When the results are averaged, the personal effect of each teacher will have contributed to the average scores earned under each of the three methods.

___ 8. If treatments were self-administered, did the researcher check on treatment compliance?

Very satisfactory 5 4 3 2 1 Very unsatisfactory ***or*** N/A I/I

Comment: Some treatments are self-administered, out of view of the researcher. For instance, an experimental group might be given a new antidepressant drug to self-administer over a period of months. The researcher could check treatment compliance by asking participants how faithful they are being in taking the drug. More elaborate checks would include instructing participants to keep a diary of their drug-taking schedule, or even conducting tests that detect the presence of the drug.

___ 9. Except for differences in the treatments, were all other conditions the same in the experimental and control groups?

Very satisfactory 5 4 3 2 1 Very unsatisfactory ***or*** N/A I/I

Comment: The results of an experiment can be influenced by many variables other than the independent variable. For instance, if experimental and control groups are treated at different times of the day or in different rooms in a building (where one room is noisy and the other is not), these factors might influence the outcome of an experiment. Researchers refer to variables such as these as *confounding variables* because they confound the interpretation of the results.

___ 10. When appropriate, have the researchers considered possible demand characteristics?

Very satisfactory 5 4 3 2 1 Very unsatisfactory ***or*** N/A I/I

Comment: If participants know (or suspect) the purpose of an experiment, their responses may be influenced by this knowledge. For instance, in a study on the effects of a film showing negative consequences of drinking alcohol, the experimental group participants might report more negative attitudes toward alcohol only because they suspect the researcher has hypothesized that this will happen. In other words, sometimes participants try to give researchers what they think the researchers expect. This is known as a *demand characteristic*. It is called this because the phenomenon operates as though a researcher is subtly demanding a certain outcome.

Certain types of measures are more prone to the effects of demand characteristics than others. Self-report measures (such as self-reported attitudes toward alcohol) are especially sensitive to them. When interpreting the results obtained with such measures, researchers should consider whether any differences are due to the demands of the experiments. One way to overcome this difficulty is to supplement self-report measures with other measures, such as reports by friends or significant others.

On the other hand, an achievement test is less sensitive to the demands of an experiment because students who do not have the skills being tested will not be successful on a test even if they want to please the researcher by producing the desired behavior. Likewise, many physical measures are insensitive to this type of influence. In an experiment on methods for reducing cocaine use, for instance, a participant will not be able to alter the results of a blood test for the presence of cocaine.

___ 11. Is the setting for the experiment natural?

Very satisfactory 5 4 3 2 1 Very unsatisfactory ***or*** N/A I/I

Comment: Sometimes, researchers conduct experiments in artificial settings. When they do this, they limit their study's *external validity*, that is, what is found in the artificial environment of an experiment may not be found in more natural settings (i.e., the finding may not be valid in a more natural setting).

Experiments conducted in laboratory settings often have poor external validity. Notice the unnatural aspects of Example 9.11.1. First, the amount and type of alcoholic beverages were assigned (rather than being selected by the participants as they would be in a natural setting). Second, the female was a cohort of the experimenters (not someone the males were actually dating). Third, the setting was a laboratory, where the males would be likely to suspect that their behavior was being monitored in some way. While the researchers have achieved a high degree of physical control over the experimental setting, they have sacrificed external validity in the process.

Example 9.11.1

Experiment with poor external validity:

A research team was interested in the effects of alcohol consumption on aggressiveness in males when dating. In the experiment, some of the males were given moderate amounts of beer to consume, while controls were given nonalcoholic beer. Then all males were observed interacting with a female cohort of the experimenters. The interactions took place in a laboratory on a college campus, and observations were made through a one-way mirror.

___ 12. Has the researcher distinguished between random selection and random assignment?

Very satisfactory 5 4 3 2 1 Very unsatisfactory ***or*** N/A I/I

Comment: The desirability of using *random selection* to obtain samples from which researchers can generalize with confidence to larger populations was discussed in Chapter 6. Such selection is highly desirable in most studies—whether they are experiments or not. *Random assignment*, on the other hand, refers to the process of assigning participants to the various treatment conditions (i.e., to the treatments, including any control condition).

Note that in any given experiment, *selection* may or may not be random. Likewise, *assignment* may or may not be random. Figure 9.12.1 illustrates the ideal situation, where first there is random selection from a population of interest to obtain a sample. This is followed by random assignment to treatment conditions.

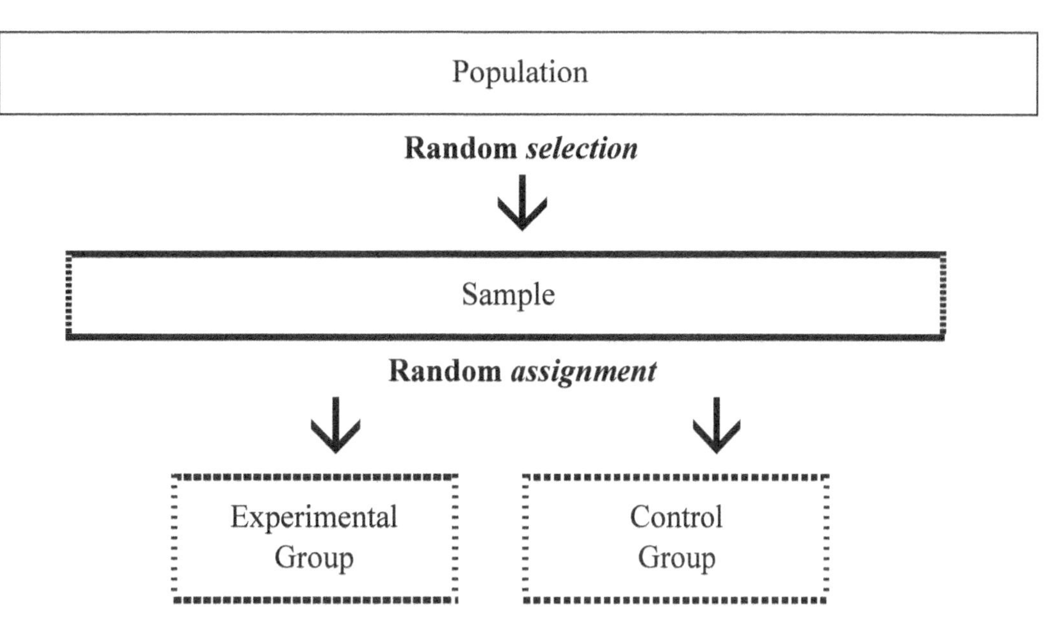

Figure 9.12.1. Ideal combination of random selection and random assignment.

When discussing the generalizability of the results of an experiment, a researcher should do so in light of the type of *selection* used. In other words, a properly selected sample (ideally, one selected at random) allows for more confidence in generalizing the results to a population. On the other hand, when discussing the comparability of the two groups, a researcher should consider the type of *assignment* used. In other words, proper assignment to a group (ideally, assignment at random) increases researchers' confidence that the two groups were initially equal—permitting a valid comparison of the outcomes of treatment and control conditions.

___ 13. Has the researcher considered attrition?

Very satisfactory 5 4 3 2 1 Very unsatisfactory ***or*** N/A I/I

Comment: The phenomenon of individuals dropping out of a study is referred to as *attrition* (sometimes called *experimental mortality*). The longer and more complex the experimental treatment, the more likely it is that some participants will drop out. This can affect the generalizability of the results because they will apply only to the types of individuals who continued to participate.

For researchers who conduct experiments, *differential attrition* can be an important source of confounding. Differential attrition refers to the possibility that those who drop out of an experimental condition are of a type different from those who drop out of a control condition. For instance, in an experiment on a weight-loss program, those in the experimental group who get discouraged by failing to lose weight may drop out. Thus, those who remain in the experimental condition are those who are more successful, leading to an overestimate of the beneficial effects of the weight-loss program.

Researchers usually cannot physically prevent attrition. However, often they can compare those who dropped out with those who remained in the study in an effort to determine whether those who remained and those who dropped out were similar in important ways. Example 9.13.1 shows a portion of a statement dealing with this matter.

Example 9.13.1[9]
Description of an attrition analysis:

The participant attrition rate in this study raised the concern that the participants successfully completing the procedure were different from those who did not in some important way that would render the results less generalizable. Thus, an attrition analysis was undertaken to determine which, if any, of a variety of participant variables could account for participant attrition. Participant variables analyzed included ages of the participants and the parents, birth order and weight, socioeconomic status, duration of prenatal health care, prenatal risk factor exposure, hours spent weekly in day care, parental ratings of quality of infant's previous night's sleep, and time elapsed since last feeding and diaper change. This analysis revealed two effects: On average, participants who completed the procedure had been fed more recently than those who did not complete the procedure..., and those who completed the procedure were slightly younger (153.5 days) than those who did not (156 days)....

___ 14. Has the researcher used ethical and politically acceptable treatments?

Very satisfactory 5 4 3 2 1 Very unsatisfactory ***or*** N/A I/I

Comment: This evaluation question is applicable primarily to experiments in applied areas such as education, clinical psychology, social work, and nursing. For instance, has the researcher used treatments to promote classroom discipline that will be acceptable to parents, teachers, and the community? Has the researcher used methods such as moderate corporal punishment by teachers, which may be unacceptable in typical classroom settings?

A low mark on this question means that the experiment is unlikely to have an impact in the applied area in which it was conducted.

---

[9] Moore, D. S., & Cocas, L. A. (2006). Perception precedes computation: Can familiarity preferences explain apparent calculation by human babies? *Developmental Psychology*, *42*, 666–678.

___ **15. Overall, was the experiment properly conducted?**

Very satisfactory 5 4 3 2 1 Very unsatisfactory ***or*** N/A I/I

Comment: Rate the overall quality of the experimental procedures on the basis of the answers to the evaluation questions in this chapter and taking into account any other concerns you may have.

Exercise for Chapter 9

Part A

Directions: Answer the following questions.

1. In an experiment, a treatment constitutes what is known as
   A. an independent variable. B. a dependent variable.

2. Which of the following is described in this chapter as being vastly superior to the other?
   A. Assigning previously existing *groups* to treatments at random.
   B. Assigning *individuals* to treatments at random.

3. Suppose a psychology professor conducted an experiment in which one of her sections of Introduction to Social Psychology was assigned to be the experimental group and the other section served as the control group during a given semester. The experimental group used computer-assisted instruction while the control group received instruction via a traditional lecture/discussion method. Although both groups are taking a course in social psychology during the same semester, the two groups might be initially different in other ways. Speculate on what some of the differences might be. (See Evaluation Question 2.)

4. In this chapter, what is described as a strength of an experimental design in which one group serves as both the treatment group and its own control group?

5. Very briefly describe how the personal effect might confound an experiment.

6. What is the name of the phenomenon in which participants may be influenced by knowledge of the purpose of an experiment?

7. Briefly explain how *random selection* differs from *random assignment*.

8. Is it possible to have *nonrandom selection* yet still have *random assignment* in an experiment? Explain.

Part B

Directions: Locate reports on two experiments on topics of interest to you. Evaluate them in light of the evaluation questions in this chapter, taking into account any other considerations and concerns you may have. Select the one to which you gave the highest overall rating, and bring it to class for discussion. Be prepared to discuss its strengths and weaknesses.

Chapter 10

Evaluating Analysis and Results Sections: Quantitative Research

This chapter discusses the evaluation of Analysis and Results sections in *quantitative research* reports. These almost always contain statistics that summarize the data that were collected, such as means, standard deviations, and correlation coefficients. These types of statistics are known as *descriptive statistics*. The Results sections of quantitative research reports also usually contain *inferential statistics*, which help in making inferences from the sample that was actually studied to the population from which the sample was drawn. It is assumed that the reader has a basic knowledge of elementary statistical methods.

Note that the evaluation of Analysis and Results sections of *qualitative research* reports is covered in the next chapter.

___ 1. When percentages are reported, are the underlying numbers of cases also reported?

Very satisfactory 5 4 3 2 1 Very unsatisfactory ***or*** N/A I/I

Comment: Percentages are very widely reported in research reports in academic journals.

When reporting percentages, it is important for researchers to also report the underlying number of cases for each percentage. Otherwise, the results can be misleading. Consider Example 10.1.1, which contains only percentages. The percentage decrease in this example seems dramatic. However, when the underlying numbers of cases (whose symbol is *n*) are shown, as in Example 10.1.2, it becomes clear that the percentage represents only a very small decrease in absolute terms (i.e., a decrease from 4 students to 2 students).

Example 10.1.1

Percentage reported without underlying number of cases (potentially misleading):

Since the end of the Cold War, interest in Russian language studies has decreased dramatically. For instance, at Zaneville Language Institute, the number of students majoring in Russian has decreased by 50% from a decade earlier.

Example 10.1.2

Percentage reported with underlying number of cases (not misleading):

Since the end of the Cold War, interest in Russian language studies has decreased dramatically. For instance, at Zaneville Language Institute, the number of students majoring in Russian has decreased by 50% from a decade earlier (n = 4 in 2002, n = 2 in 2012).

___2. Are means reported only for approximately symmetrical distributions?

Very satisfactory 5 4 3 2 1 Very unsatisfactory ***or*** N/A I/I

Comment: The *mean*, which is the most commonly reported average, should be used only when a distribution is *not* highly skewed. In other words, it should be used only when a distribution is approximately symmetrical.

A skewed distribution is one in which there are some extreme scores on one side of the distribution (such as some very high scores without some very low scores to counterbalance them). Example 10.2.1 shows a skewed distribution. It is skewed because there is a very high score of 310, which is not balanced out by a very low score at the lower end of the distribution of scores. This is known as a distribution that is *skewed to the right.*[1] The mean, which is supposed to represent the central tendency of the entire group of scores, has been pulled up by a single very high score, resulting in a mean of 82.45, which is higher than all of the scores except the highest one (the score of 310).

Example 10.2.1

A skewed distribution (skewed to the right) and a misleading mean:

Scores: 55, 55, 56, 57, 58, 60, 61, 63, 66, 66, 310
Mean = 82.45, standard deviation = 75.57

The raw scores for which a mean was calculated are very seldom included in research reports, which makes it impossible to inspect for skewedness. However, a couple of simple computations using only the mean and standard deviation (which are usually reported) can reveal whether the mean was misapplied to a distribution that is highly skewed to the right. These are the calculations:

1. Round the mean and standard deviation to whole numbers (to keep the computations simple). Thus, the rounded mean is 82, and the rounded standard deviation is 76 for Example 10.2.1.
2. Multiply the standard deviation by 2 (i.e., $76 \times 2 = 152$).
3. *SUBTRACT* the result of Step 2 from the mean (i.e., $82 - 152 = -70$).

[1] A distribution that is skewed to the right is also said to have a *positive skew*.

If the result of Step 3 is lower than the lowest possible score, which is usually zero, the distribution is highly skewed to the right.[2] (In this example, –70 is much lower than zero.) This indicates that the mean was applied to a distribution that is skewed to the right, resulting in a misleading value for an average (i.e., an average that is misleadingly high).[3] This type of inappropriate selection of an average is rather common, perhaps because researchers often compute the mean and standard deviation for a set of scores without first considering whether the distribution of scores is skewed.

It is also easy to detect the misapplication of the mean to describe a distribution that is highly *skewed to the left*.[4] Example 10.2.2 illustrates this, with a very low score of 3 without a very high score on the right to balance it out. This distribution has a mean score of 54.54, which is lower than all the other scores in the distribution except for the extremely low score of 3. Thus, 54.54 does not appropriately represent the central tendency of the distribution.

Example 10.2.2

A skewed distribution (skewed to the left) and a misleading mean:

Scores: 3, 55, 55, 56, 57, 58, 60, 61, 63, 66, 66

Mean = 54.54, standard deviation = 17.56

When the raw scores are not available, a consumer of research can determine if the distribution is skewed to the left by using the mean and standard deviation in the following steps, which are illustrated for Example 10.2.2:

1. Round the mean and standard deviations to whole numbers (to keep the computations simple). Thus, the rounded mean is 55, and the rounded standard deviation is 18 for Example 10.2.2.
2. Multiply the standard deviation by 2 (i.e., 18 × 2 = 36).
3. *ADD* the result of Step 2 to the mean (i.e., 55 + 36 = 91).

If the result of Step 3 is higher than the highest score, the distribution is highly skewed to the left. (In this example, the result of Step 3 is 91, which is higher than the highest score of 66.) This indicates that the mean was misapplied to a distribution highly skewed to the left, resulting in a misleading low value for an average.

---

[2] In a normal, symmetrical distribution, there are 3 standard deviation units on each side of the mean. Thus, there should be 3 standard deviation units on both sides of the mean in a distribution that is not skewed. In this example, there are not even 2 standard deviation units to the left of the mean (because the standard deviation was multiplied by 2). Even without understanding this theory, a consumer of research can still apply the simple steps described here to identify the misapplication of the mean. Note that there are precise statistical methods for detecting a skew. However, for their use to be possible, the original scores would be needed, and those are almost never available to consumers of research.

[3] This procedure will not detect all highly skewed distributions. If the result of Step 3 is lower than the lowest score obtained by any participant, the distribution is also skewed. However, researchers seldom report the lowest score obtained by participants.

[4] A distribution that is skewed to the left is said to have a *negative skew*.

If a consumer of research detects that a mean has been computed for a highly skewed distribution by performing the two sets of calculations described, there is little that can be done to correct it short of contacting the researcher to request the raw scores.[5] If this is not feasible, the mean should be interpreted with great caution, and the research report should be given a low mark on this evaluation question.

___ 3. If any differences are statistically significant and small, have the researchers noted that they are small?

Very satisfactory 5 4 3 2 1 Very unsatisfactory ***or*** N/A I/I

Comment: Statistically significant differences are sometimes very small. (See Appendix C for an explanation of this point.) When this is the case, it is a good idea for a researcher to point this out. Obviously, a very small but statistically significant difference will be interpreted differently from a large and statistically significant difference.

Example 10.3.1 illustrates how a significant but small difference might be pointed out.[6]

Example 10.3.1

Description of a small but statistically significant difference:

Although the difference between the means of the experimental group (M = 24.55) and control group (M = 23.65) was statistically significant ($t = 2.075, p < .05$), the small size of the difference, in absolute terms, suggests that the effects of the experimental treatment were weak.

This evaluation question is important in that researchers sometimes incorrectly imply that because a difference is statistically significant, it is necessarily large and important.

___ 4. Is the Results section a cohesive essay?

Very satisfactory 5 4 3 2 1 Very unsatisfactory ***or*** N/A I/I

Comment: The Results section should be an essay—not just a collection of statistics. In other words, researchers should describe results in paragraphs, each of which describes some aspect of the results. These paragraphs generally will contain statistics. The essay usually should be organized around the research hypotheses, research questions, or research purposes. See the example under the next guideline.

---

[5] With the raw scores, a consumer of research could compute the *median*, which is the appropriate average to use with skewed distributions. To obtain the median for a set of scores, put them in order from low to high and count to the middle score, which is the median. In Example 10.2.2, there are 11 scores, and the middle score is 58, which is the median. Notice that this is in the center of the set of scores.

[6] An increasingly popular statistic, *effect size*, is designed to draw readers' attention to the size of any significant difference. In general terms, it indicates by how many standard deviations two groups differ from each other. Unfortunately, its use is not very widespread to date.

___ 5. Does the researcher refer back to the research hypotheses, purposes, or questions originally stated in the introduction?

Very satisfactory 5 4 3 2 1 Very unsatisfactory ***or*** N/A I/I

Comment: This guideline may not be applicable to a very short research report with a single hypothesis, question, or purpose. When there are several of these, however, readers should be shown how different elements of the results relate to the specific hypotheses, questions, or purposes, as illustrated in Example 10.5.1. The example refers to three research purposes, which are briefly restated in the narrative. The tables referred to in the example are not shown here.

Example 10.5.1

Results discussed in terms of research purposes stated earlier in the report:

The first purpose was to determine adolescent students' estimates of the frequency of use of illicit drugs by students-at-large in their high schools. Table 1 shows the percentages for each....

Regarding the second purpose (estimates of illicit drug use by close friends), the percentages in Table 2 clearly indicate....

Finally, results relating to the third purpose are shown in Table 3. Since the purpose was to determine the differences between....

___ 6. When there are a number of related statistics, have they been presented in a table?

Very satisfactory 5 4 3 2 1 Very unsatisfactory ***or*** N/A I/I

Comment: Even when there are only a small number of related statistics, a table can be helpful. For instance, consider Example 10.6.1, in which percentages and numbers of cases (n) are presented in a paragraph. Compare it with Example 10.6.2, in which the same 10 percentages are reported in tabular form. Clearly, the tabular form is easier to follow.

Example 10.6.1[7]

Too many statistics presented in a paragraph (compare with Example 10.6.2, which presents the same statistics in a table):

Two percent of the girls (n = 8) and 2% of the boys (n = 8) reported that they were "Far too skinny." Boys and girls were also identical in response to the choice "A little skinny" (8%, n = 41 for girls and 8%, n = 34 for boys). For "Just right," a larger percentage of boys (76%, n = 337) than girls (70%, n = 358) responded. For "A little fat," the responses were 18% (n = 92) and 13% (n = 60) for girls and boys, respectively. Also, a slightly higher percentage of girls than

[7] Adapted from Erling, A., & Hwang, C. P. (2004). Body-esteem in Swedish 10-year-old children. *Perceptual and Motor Skills*, *99*, 437–444. In the research report, the statistics are reported in tabular form, as recommended here.

boys reported being "Far too fat" with 2% (n = 12) for girls and 1% (n = 6) for boys.

Example 10.6.2

Table 1

Answers to question on self-perceived weight

	Girls		Boys	
Answer	%	*n*	%	*n*
Far too skinny	2	8	2	8
A little skinny	8	41	8	34
Just right	70	358	76	337
A little fat	18	92	13	60
Far too fat	2	12	1	6

___ **7. If there are tables, are their highlights discussed in the narrative of the Results section?**

Very satisfactory 5 4 3 2 1 Very unsatisfactory ***or*** N/A I/I

Comment: Researchers should point out important highlights of statistical tables, as illustrated in Example 10.7.1, which shows part of the discussion of the statistics in Example 10.6.2. Note that only *highlights* of the statistics should be presented. To repeat them all in paragraph form would be redundant.

When there are large tables, pointing out the highlights can be especially helpful for consumers of the research.

Example 10.7.1[8]

Highlights of Example 10.6.2 pointed out:

The same percentage of boys as girls (10%) perceived themselves as a little or far too skinny, while 20% of the girls and 14% of the boys perceived themselves as a little or far too fat (see Table 1). Of the 104 girls who perceived themselves as fat (a little fat or far too fat), only....

___ **8. Have the researchers presented descriptive statistics before presenting the results of inferential tests?**

Very satisfactory 5 4 3 2 1 Very unsatisfactory ***or*** N/A I/I

Comment: Descriptive statistics include frequencies, percentages, averages (usually the mean or median), and measures of variability (usually the standard deviation or interquartile range). In addition, correlation coefficients (usually the Pearson r) describe the direction and strength of relationships.

[8] Adapted from Erling, A., & Hwang, C. P. (2004). Body-esteem in Swedish 10-year-old children. *Perceptual and Motor Skills*, *99*, 437–444. In the research report, the statistics are reported in tabular form, as recommended here.

Inferential statistics determine the probability that any differences among descriptive statistics are due to chance (random sampling error). Obviously, it makes no sense to discuss the results of a test on descriptive statistics unless those descriptive statistics have first been presented. Failure on this evaluation question is very rare.

___ **9. Overall, is the presentation of the results comprehensible?**

Very satisfactory 5 4 3 2 1 Very unsatisfactory ***or*** N/A I/I

Comment: Even when the analysis is complex and advanced statistical methods have been applied, the essay that describes the results should be comprehensible to any intelligent layperson. Specifically, the essay should describe the results conceptually using everyday language while presenting the statistical results for consumers of research who wish to consider them.

___ **10. Overall, is the presentation of the results adequate?**

Very satisfactory 5 4 3 2 1 Very unsatisfactory ***or*** N/A I/I

Comment: Rate this evaluation question after considering your answers to the earlier ones in this chapter and taking into account any additional considerations and concerns you may have.

Exercise for Chapter 10

Part A

Directions: Answer the following questions.

1. When reporting percentages, what else is it important for researchers to present?

2. Should the mean be used to report the average of a highly skewed distribution?

3. Suppose you read that the mean equals 10.0 and the standard deviation equals 6.0. Is the distribution skewed? (Assume that the lowest possible score is zero.) Explain.

4. Are statistically significant differences always large differences?

5. Should the Results section be an essay *or* should it be only a collection of statistics?

6. According to this chapter, is it ever desirable to restate hypotheses that were originally stated in the introduction of a research report? Explain.

7. If statistical results are presented in a table, should all the entries in the table be discussed in the narrative? Explain.

8. Should "descriptive statistics" *or* "inferential tests" be reported first in Results sections?

Part B

Directions: Locate several quantitative research reports of interest to you in academic journals. Read them, and evaluate the descriptions of the results in light of the evaluation questions in this chapter, taking into account any other considerations and concerns you may have. Select the one to which you gave the highest overall rating, and bring it to class for discussion. Be prepared to discuss its strengths and weaknesses.

Chapter 11

Evaluating Analysis and Results Sections: Qualitative Research

Because human judgment is central in the analysis of qualitative data, there is much more subjectivity in the analysis of qualitative data than in the analysis of quantitative data. (See Chapter 10 for evaluation questions for quantitative Analysis and Results sections of research reports.) Consult Appendix A for additional information on the differences between qualitative and quantitative research.

___ 1. Were the data analyzed independently by two or more individuals?

Very satisfactory 5 4 3 2 1 Very unsatisfactory ***or*** N/A I/I

Comment: As a general rule, the results of qualitative research are considered more dependable when the responses of participants are independently analyzed by two or more individuals (i.e., two or more individuals initially code and/or categorize the responses without consulting with each other). Then, they compare the results of their analyses and discuss any discrepancies in an effort to reach a consensus. Doing this assures consumers of research that the results represent more than just the impressions of one individual, which might be idiosyncratic. Examples 11.1.1, 11.1.2, and 11.1.3 illustrate how this process might be described in a research report.

Example 11.1.1[1]

Independent analysis by two researchers:

Two independent research psychologists developed a list of *domains* or *topic areas* based on the content of the discussions and the focus group questions used to organize information into similar topics. Once each reviewer had independently identified their domains, the two reviewers compared their separate lists of domains until consensus was reached.

---

[1] Williams, J. K., Wyatt, G. E., Resell, J., Peterson, J., & Asuan-O'Brien, A. (2004). Psychosocial issues among gay- and non-gay-identifying HIV-seropositive African American and Latino MSM. *Cultural Diversity and Ethnic Minority Psychology*, *10*, 268–286.

Example 11.1.2[2]

Independent analysis by three researchers (italics added for emphasis):

The interview notes were analyzed by three raters: myself and two doctoral students.... Each quote from the notes was assigned a descriptive category according to its content. The notes were organized into groups with the same category labels. Some similar groups were combined under inclusive categories. The main categories that were derived from the interviews, the coping strategies, mechanisms, and resources were then defined. In the next stage, the information from the interviews was coded according to the defined categories, evaluated, and summarized to describe the realities as accurately as possible. *Each of the three raters independently analyzed the type of coping strategies and categories. Any disagreement between raters was discussed and resolved.* The interrater reliability was high.

Example 11.1.3[3]

Independent analysis by two researchers:

Using a grounded theory approach, we used standard, qualitative procedures to code the data (Strauss & Corbin, 1998). Two coders, working independently, read a transcript of clients' unedited answers to each question and identified phenomena in the text that were deemed responsive to the question and thus, in the opinion of the coder, should be regarded as relevant data for inclusion in the analysis. Phenomena included all phrases or statements conveying meaningful ideas, events, objects, and actions. If both coders selected the same phrase or statement in the answer to a given question, then it was counted as an agreement. Overall, percent agreement between coders averaged 89% (±6 *SD*) for this first step. Disagreements were resolved through discussion and consensus.

___ **2. Did the researchers seek feedback from experienced individuals and auditors before finalizing the results?**

Very satisfactory 5 4 3 2 1 Very unsatisfactory ***or*** N/A I/I

Comment: Seeking feedback helps to ensure the trustworthiness of the results. Example 11.2.1 is drawn from a report of research on incarcerated young men. The researchers had their preliminary results reviewed by two other individuals who had experienced incarceration (independent experienced individuals).

---

[2] Westman, M. (2004). Strategies for coping with business trips: A qualitative exploratory study. *International Journal of Stress Management*, *11*, 167–176.

[3] Beitel, M., Genova, M., Schuman-Olivier, Z., Arnold, R., Avants, S. K., & Margolin, A. (2007). Reflections by inner-city drug users on a Buddhist-based spirituality-focused therapy: A qualitative study. *American Journal of Orthopsychiatry*, *77*, 1–9.

Example 11.2.1[4]

Feedback from independent experienced individuals:

Finally, the data summary was reviewed by two individuals with a personal history of incarceration who were not involved in the data analytic process for critique of the face validity of the findings. Their feedback was incorporated into the discussion of our findings.

Often, researchers seek feedback on their preliminary results from outside experts who were not involved in conducting the research. The technical title for such a person in qualitative research is *auditor*. Example 11.2.2 describes the work of an auditor in a research project.

Example 11.2.2[5]

Feedback from a content-area expert (i.e., auditor):

At three separate points..., the work of the analysis team was reviewed by an auditor. The first point came after domains had been agreed upon, the second point came after core ideas had been identified, and the third point came after the cross-analysis. In each case, the auditor made suggestions to the team regarding the names and ideas the team was working on. Adjustments were made after the team reached consensus on the feedback given by the auditor. Examples of feedback given by the auditor included suggestions on the wording of domain and category names and a request for an increased amount of specificity in the core ideas put forth by the team members. The auditor was a Caucasian female faculty member in the social psychology discipline whose research is focused in the area of domestic violence.

___ 3. Did the researchers seek feedback from the participants (i.e., use member checking) before finalizing the results?

Very satisfactory 5 4 3 2 1 Very unsatisfactory ***or*** N/A I/I

Comment: As indicated in the discussion of Evaluation Question 2, seeking feedback helps to ensure the trustworthiness of the results. When researchers seek feedback on their preliminary results from the participants in the research, the process is called *member checking*. Using member checking is not always feasible, especially with very young participants and participants with limited cognitive abilities. The authors of Example 11.3.1 used member checking.

---

[4] Seal, D. W., Belcher, L., Morrow, K., Eldridge, G., Binson, D., Kacanek, D., ... Simms, R. (2004). A qualitative study of substance use and sexual behavior among 18- to 29-year-old men while incarcerated in the United States. *Health Education & Behavior, 31*, 775–789.

[5] Wettersten, K. B. et al. (2004). Freedom through self-sufficiency: A qualitative examination of the impact of domestic violence on the working lives of women in shelter. *Journal of Counseling Psychology, 51*, 447–462.

Example 11.3.1[6]

Feedback from "members" (i.e., member checking by participants):

To ensure methodological rigor, trustworthiness (Oktay, 2004; Straus & Corbin, 1998) of the data involved member (participant) checking to establish that the reconstructions were credible and that the findings were faithful to participants' experiences. Participants were provided written and oral summaries of their responses and given opportunities for correction, verification, and clarification through follow-up letters, telephone contacts, and interviews. For example, upon receiving their transcribed interviews, researchers told participants, "As you read through your transcript, you may want to make notes that would further clarify what was said or address an area that was not originally discussed." And in the follow-up interview, participants were asked, "Are there any changes or additional comments that you would like to discuss in regard to the study's findings?" Additionally, researchers conducted ongoing peer debriefing to review their audit trail regarding the research process.

___ **4. Did the researchers name the method of analysis they used and provide a reference for it?**

Very satisfactory 5 4 3 2 1 Very unsatisfactory ***or*** N/A I/I

Comment: Various methods for analyzing qualitative data have been suggested. Researchers should name the particular method they followed. Often, they name it and provide one or more references where additional information can be obtained. Examples 11.4.1 and 11.4.2 illustrate this for two widely used methods (the grounded theory method and the consensual qualitative approach).

Example 11.4.1[7]

Naming grounded theory as the method of analysis with references for more information on the method (bold italics added for emphasis):

According to Strauss and Corbin (1998), ***grounded theory*** is a "general methodology for developing theory that is grounded in data systematically gathered and analyzed" (p. 158). This approach uses "data triangulation" (Janesick, 1998) with multiple data sources (e.g., different families and family members, different groups and facilitators) and a "constant comparative method" (Glaser, 1967) by continually examining the analytic results with the raw data. The analysis proceeded in steps. First, a "start list" consisting of 42 descriptive codes was created on the basis of ongoing community immersion and fieldwork as well as the

[6] Anderson, K. M., Danis, F. S., & Havig, K. (2011). Adult daughters of battered women: Recovery and posttraumatic growth following childhood adversity. *Families in Society: The Journal of Contemporary Social Services*, *92*, 154–160.

[7] Weine, S., Feetham, S., Kulauzovic, Y., Knafl, K., Besic, S., Klebic, A., ... Pavkovic, I. (2006). A family beliefs framework for socially and culturally specific preventative interventions with refugee youths and families. *American Journal of Orthopsychiatry*, *76*, 1–9.

perspectives of family beliefs (Weine, 2001b) and the prevention and access intervention framework used to develop the CAFES intervention (Weine, 1998). The codes addressed a variety of topics pertaining to refugee families suggested by prior empirical and conceptual work. Texts were coded with only these codes, and they were supplemented with memos for any items of interest that did not match the code list. Out of the start list of 42 codes, 3 codes focused on adapting family beliefs.

Example 11.4.2[8]

Naming consensual qualitative research as the method of analysis with references for more information on the method (bold italics added for emphasis):

We used ***consensual qualitative research (CQR)*** methodology for this study because of its ability to evoke detailed data pertaining to people's phenomenological or subjective experiences (Hill et al., 2005; Hill et al., 1997). The team of interviewers and primary raters consisted of two African American female doctoral students in counseling psychology and one African American female undergraduate student in psychology. An Asian American male faculty member in counseling psychology served as the internal auditor. Two of the investigators had previously implemented CQR: They trained the other team members in the application of the method. As recommended by Hill et al. (2005), we included an external auditor who was not involved in the study to review the work and provide feedback on the analysis process: She was a Pakistani American female doctoral student in counseling psychology.

___ **5. Did the researchers state *specifically* how the method of analysis was applied?**

Very satisfactory 5 4 3 2 1 Very unsatisfactory ***or*** N/A I/I

Comment: The previous evaluation question suggests that the particular method of analysis should be identified and that references for it should be provided. This evaluation question asks if the application of the method selected is described in sufficient detail. At a minimum, the steps followed in the analysis of the data should be described, as in Example 11.5.1. Note that in some reports of qualitative research, the descriptions are quite detailed.

[8] Sánchez, F. J., Liu, W. M., Leathers, L., Goins, J., & Vilain, E. (2011). The subjective experience of social class and upward mobility among African American men in graduate school. *Psychology of Men & Masculinity, 12*, 368–382.

Example 11.5.1[9]

Describing the steps used in the analysis of qualitative data:

We analyzed transcribed data using a "code mapping" procedure as described by Knodel (1993). Code mapping requires that researchers read the transcript to identify sections that are relevant to the research questions and get a sense of possible categories within the data. A second reading is used to produce initial categories of words, phrases, and sentences. Cyclical reading and coding continues until final categories are derived from the data. In this analysis, all four authors read each focus group transcript independently to familiarize themselves with the data. Then three of the four authors (the social work assistant professors and doctoral student) independently coded participants' statements into initial categories, based on the criteria of relevance to the research question, clarity of expression, and consistency with other included statements. These authors then presented the resulting categories to each other during discussion. Agreement for assignment of statements to initial categories across coders ranged from 85% to 93%. Conjoint cyclical coding and additional discussion resulted in consensus on all categories and identification of illustrative quotations. These categories and quotations were reviewed by the additional author (the adoption consultant) to minimize researcher bias (Piercy & Hertlein, 2005). No changes were recommended.

In order to parsimoniously represent the common voice of participants, we chose quotations that capture broadly endorsed and supported positions for inclusion in this article. We also included quotations that express significant dissonant positions and identified them as such, in order to provide a balanced and accurate account of participants' preferences.

___ 6. Did the researchers self-disclose their backgrounds?

Very satisfactory 5 4 3 2 1 Very unsatisfactory ***or*** N/A I/I

Comment: Sometimes, qualitative researchers disclose their own background characteristics as they relate to the variables under investigation. For instance, a researcher studying the social dynamics of men with HIV might reveal their own HIV status and that of their significant others. This is done in an effort to "clear the air" regarding any personal points of view and biases that might impact the researcher's analysis of the data.

Example 11.6.1 shows a portion of such a disclosure. The researchers included the statement in their Analysis section under the subheading Author Biases.

---

[9] Mooradian, J. K., Hock, R. M., Jackson, R., & Timm, T. M. (2011). What couples who adopt children from child welfare want professionals to know about supporting their marriages. *Families in Society: The Journal of Contemporary Social Services*, *92*, 390–396.

Example 11.6.1[10]

Researchers' self-disclosure:

Mary Lee Nelson is a professor of counseling psychology. She came from a lower middle-, working-class background, was the first in her family to pursue higher education, and had many of the experiences described by the research participants. This background provided her with important insights about the data. In addition, it might have biased her expectations about what participants' experiences would be. She expected to hear stories of financial hardship, social confusion, loneliness, and challenges with personal and career identity development. Matt Englar-Carlson is a counseling psychologist and currently an associate professor of counselor education. He has a strong interest in new developments in social class theory. He comes from a middle-class, educated family background. He came to the study with expectations that findings might conform to the social class worldview model, as developed by Liu (2001). Sandra C. Tierney is a recent graduate of a doctoral program in....

___ 7. Are the results of qualitative studies adequately supported with examples of quotations or descriptions of observations?

Very satisfactory 5 4 3 2 1 Very unsatisfactory ***or*** N/A I/I

Comment: Qualitative researchers typically report few, if any, statistics in the Results section. Instead, they report on the themes and categories that emerged from the data, while looking for patterns that might have implications for theory development. Instead of statistics, quotations from participants or descriptions of observations of the participants' behaviors are used to support the general statements regarding results.[11] This is illustrated in Example 11.7.1, in which a quotation is used to support a finding. As is typical in qualitative studies, researchers set off the quotation in block style (i.e., indented on left and right).

Example 11.7.1[12]

Results of a qualitative study supported with quotations:

Although education was important to these men, there were barriers that they encountered in working toward their degrees, including expectations that they would fail and intrinsic pressure to succeed:

> I am proud to be a Black man, and I am proud to have gotten where I am, but I'm real conscious of the fact that people are expecting less of me. There are days

---

[10] Nelson, M. L., Englar-Carlson, M., Tierney, S. C., & Hau, J. M. (2006). Class jumping into academia: Multiple identities for counseling academics. *Journal of Counseling Psychology*, *53*, 1–14.

[11] The use of extensive quotations is a technique used to produce what qualitative researchers refer to as *thick descriptions*.

[12] Sánchez, F. J., Liu, W. M., Leathers, L., Goins, J., & Vilain, E. (2011). The subjective experience of social class and upward mobility among African American men in graduate school. *Psychology of Men & Masculinity*, *12*, 368–382.

> where I go at 150%, and there are days where I am tired and I can't go that hard; I can have great class presentations, and I can have a crappy presentation sometimes. When I am on a bad day or when I have a bad presentation—those stay with me longer than the good ones because of the fact that there are very few of us [in graduate school] and, thus, it's a burden that we've got to protect...we got to come tight with our game. And, not all the time I'm feeling that.

Consumers of qualitative research should make judgments as to how well the quotations illustrate and support the research findings.

___ 8. Are appropriate statistics reported (especially for demographics)?

Very satisfactory 5 4 3 2 1 Very unsatisfactory ***or*** N/A I/I

Comment: The main description of the results of qualitative research is relatively free of statistics. However, statistical matters often arise when the results are written up. This could be as simple as reporting the numbers of cases (whose statistical symbol is *n*). For instance, instead of reporting that "*some students* were observed with their heads down on their desks," it might be better to report that "*six students* were observed with their heads down on their desks." Too much emphasis on exact numbers, however, can be distracting in a qualitative research report. Hence, this evaluation question should be applied judiciously.

One of the most appropriate uses of statistics in qualitative research is to describe the demographics of the participants. When there are a large number of demographic statistics, it is best to present them in a statistical table, which makes it easier for consumers of research to scan for relevant information. Example 11.8.1 shows a table of demographics presented in a qualitative research report.

Example 11.8.1[13]

Demographic statistics in qualitative research reported in a table:

Table 1

Focus Group Participant Demographics (N = 28)

Characteristics	*n*	%
Gender		
Men	21	75
Women	7	25
Age		
16–20	2	7
21–30	7	25
31–40	9	32
41–50	8	29
51–54	2	7

(continued)

[13] Ames, N., Hancock, T. U., & Behnke, A. O. (2011). Latino church leaders and domestic violence: Attitudes and knowledge. *Families in Society: The Journal of Contemporary Social Services*, *92*, 161–167.

Table1 *Focus Group Participant Demographics (N = 28)* (continued)

Characteristics	*n*	%
Marital status		
Married	20	71
Single	8	29
Income		
< $10,001	7	25
$10,001–$20,000	8	29
$20,001–$30,000	8	29
$30,001–$40,000	4	14
> $40,000	1	3
Years of U.S. residence		
2–5	8	29
6–10	9	32
11–15	4	14
16–20	6	21
21–25	1	4
Place of residence		
Rural	20	71
Urban	8	29
Employment		
Construction worker	11	39
Factory worker	5	18
No outside employment	6	21
Other[a]	6	21
Education		
HS diploma/GED	17	61
No HS diploma	7	25
Some college	4	14

[a]Examples include driver, caterer, baker, dry cleaner, nanny, and housecleaner.

Example 11.8.2 illustrates the reporting of demographic statistics in the narrative of a qualitative research report.[14]

Example 11.8.2[15]

Demographic statistics reported in qualitative research:

A purposive sample of 8 convicted child molesters, 7 European Americans and 1 Latino, aged 36 to 52 (M = 44.0, SD = 6.4), was recruited from an outpatient treatment facility for sex offenders in a northeastern urban community.... Four men were single; the others were either separated (n = 2) or divorced (n = 2); 3 indicated being gay or bisexual. Participants' educational levels were GED (n = 1), high school graduate (n = 2), some college (n = 3), some graduate work (n = 1), and master's degree (n = 1). The median annual income was $15,000–$20,000.

[14] Demographic statistics are sometimes reported in the subsection on Participants in the Method section of a research report. Other times, they are reported in the Results section.

[15] Schaefer, B. M., Friedlander, M. L., Blustein, D. L., & Maruna, S. (2004). The work lives of child molesters: A phenomenological perspective. *Journal of Counseling Psychology*, *51*, 226–239.

___ 9. Overall, is the Results section clearly organized?

Very satisfactory 5 4 3 2 1 Very unsatisfactory ***or*** N/A I/I

Comment: The Results sections of qualitative research reports are often quite long. By using subheadings throughout the Results sections, researchers can help guide their readers through sometimes complex information. Example 11.9.1 shows the major headings (in bold) and subheadings (in italics) used to help readers through a long Results section of a qualitative research report.

Example 11.9.1[16]

*Major headings (in **bold**) and subheadings (in italics) used in a long Results section of a qualitative research report*:

Results

The Aboriginal Perspective: Cultural Factors That Serve As Barriers to Rehabilitation

The strength of the local and family hierarchy

Aboriginal fatalism

The Non-Aboriginal Perspective: Unhelpful Stereotypes

Fear of Aboriginal hostility

The self-sufficiency stereotype

Motivational stereotypes

The internal strife stereotype

___ 10. Overall, is the presentation of the results adequate?

Very satisfactory 5 4 3 2 1 Very unsatisfactory ***or*** N/A I/I

Comment: Rate this evaluation question after considering your answers to the earlier ones in this chapter and any additional considerations and concerns you may have. You may also want to raise issues based on the material in Appendix B in this book.

---

[16] Kendall, E., & Marshall, C. A. (2004). Factors that prevent equitable access to rehabilitation for Aboriginal Australians with disabilities: The need for culturally safe rehabilitation. *Rehabilitation Psychology*, *49*, 5–13.

Exercise for Chapter 11

Part A

Directions: Answer the following questions.

1. When there are two or more individuals analyzing the data, what does *independently analyzed* mean?

2. What is the technical name of content-area experts who review preliminary research results for qualitative researchers?

3. What is the name of the process by which researchers seek feedback on their preliminary results from the participants in the research?

4. A researcher engages in self-disclosure in an effort to do what?

5. The results of qualitative studies should be supported with what type of material (instead of statistics)?

6. What is one of the most appropriate uses of statistics in qualitative research?

7. Because the Results sections of qualitative research reports are often quite long, what can researchers do to help guide readers?

Part B

Directions: Locate a qualitative research report of interest to you.[17] Read it, and evaluate the description of the results in light of the evaluation questions in this chapter, taking into account any other considerations and concerns you may have. Bring it to class for discussion, and be prepared to discuss both its strengths and weaknesses.

---

[17] Researchers who conduct qualitative research often mention that it is qualitative in the titles or abstracts of their reports. Thus, to locate examples of qualitative research using an electronic database, it is often advantageous to use *qualitative* as a search term.

Notes

Chapter 12

Evaluating Discussion Sections

The last section of a research article typically has the heading Discussion. However, expect to see variations such as Discussion and Conclusions, Conclusions and Implications, or Summary and Implications.

___ 1. In long articles, do the researchers briefly summarize the purpose and results at the beginning of the Discussion section?

Very satisfactory 5 4 3 2 1 Very unsatisfactory ***or*** N/A I/I

Comment: A summary at this point in a long research article reminds readers of the main focus of the research and its major findings. Often, such a summary begins by referring to the main research hypotheses, purposes, or questions addressed by the research. Example 12.1.1 shows the beginning of the first paragraph of a Discussion section that does this.

Example 12.1.1[1]

Beginning of a Discussion section that reminds readers of the purpose of the research:

The aim of this study was to examine public opinion about primary schools in Turkey. According to the results of the study, the public image of these schools was below average. This result does not support the anticipated positive image of schools in Turkey. Because Turkey is a rapidly developing nation with the largest population of young people in Europe....

The Discussion section of a lengthy research report should also often reiterate the highlights of the findings of the study. Complex results should be summarized in order that readers be reminded of the most important findings. Example 12.1.2 shows a portion of such a summary of results. Note that specific statistics (previously reported in the Results sections of quantitative research reports) do not ordinarily need to be repeated in such a summary.

[1] Ereş, F. (2011). Image of Turkish basic schools: A reflection from the province of Ankara. *The Journal of Educational Research, 104*, 431–441.

Example 12.1.2[2]

Portion of a summary of results in the Discussion section of a research article:

In our analysis of a French adult sample, regular informal caregivers with the highest burden scores reported significantly worse physical and mental health, and, in particular, more cognitive impairment than did people not having any dependent elderly individuals in their social sphere. Conversely, the caregivers with the lowest burdens reported better perceived health status and less depressive symptoms....

___ 2. Do the researchers acknowledge specific methodological limitations?

Very satisfactory 5 4 3 2 1 Very unsatisfactory ***or*** N/A I/I

Comment: Although the methodological limitations (i.e., weaknesses) may be discussed at any point in a research report, they are often discussed under the subheading Limitations within the Discussion section at the end of research reports.

The two most common types of limitations are weaknesses in measurement (i.e., observation or instrumentation) and weaknesses in sampling.

Examples 12.2.1, 12.2.2, and 12.2.3 show portions of descriptions of limitations that appeared in Discussion sections. Note that these limitations are important considerations in assessing the validity of the results of the studies.

Example 12.2.1[3]

Acknowledgment of limitations in a Discussion section:

These survey findings, of course, have numerous limitations, the most important one being that the findings are based on one school in one community and, thus, are not representative of other rural communities. Moreover, despite the reassurance of confidentiality, students might not have felt secure enough to tell the truth about their drug use and therefore might have minimized their use. Finally, as indicated in the literature, young people who have a drug problem, such as the use of methamphetamines, are likely to drop out and not be found among the high school student population.

Example 12.2.2[4]

Acknowledgment of limitations in a Discussion section:

Finally, the limitations of this study should be noted. First, the sample size in this study was small. Future studies should examine a larger sample in order to

---

[2] Buyck, J.-F., Bonnaud, S., Boumendil, A., Andrieu, S., Bonefant, S., Goldberg, M., ... Ankri, J. (2011). Informal caregiving and self-reported mental and physical health: Results from the Gazel Cohort Study. *American Journal of Public Health, 101*, 1971–1979.

[3] Mitchell, J., & Schmidt, G. (2011). The importance of local research for policy and practice: A rural Canadian study. *Journal of Social Work Practice in the Addictions, 11*, 150–162.

[4] Kuroda, Y., & Sakurai, S. (2011). Social goal orientations, interpersonal stress, and depressive symptoms among early adolescents in Japan: A test of the diathesis-stress model using the trichotomous framework of social goal orientations. *Journal of Early Adolescence, 31*, 300–322.

enhance the statistical power of the results. Second, we relied on self-reported scales to assess interpersonal stress...an alternative method, such as interviews, may yield a more objective assessment. Third, because the current study used a community sample of adolescents and did not examine clinically depressed adolescents, we must be cautious about generalizing the present findings to clinical samples.

Example 12.2.3[5]

Acknowledgment of limitations in a Discussion section:

There are several limitations to the generalizability and validity of the conclusions that can be drawn from this study. First, other variables that were not included in the present models may be better predictors of mathematics growth or may explain the observed relationships among the included variables and mathematics growth. Most important, because this was a correlational study, it is impossible to draw causal inferences from the results of the study. Therefore, any student effects reported in this study are correlational in nature, and manipulation of the variables used in this study may or may not produce similar results.

In Example 12.2.4, the researchers discuss strengths of their study before discussing limitations. This is especially appropriate when the study has special strengths to be pointed out to the readers.

Example 12.2.4[6]

Limitations discussed after strengths are described:

The study design is a strength. It utilized a national panel study with 2-year follow-ups spanning 8 years. With it we were able to examine report stability for use, age of onset, and logical consistency for the same youths. Furthermore, this is the first study to examine such measures of stability for marijuana use across nearly a decade of self-reported use. However, although marijuana use is illicit, the findings here would likely vary greatly from that of other illicit drug self-reports.

One limitation of this study is that the phrasing of the ever-use questions changed slightly during 1–2 survey years. These changes could have affected....

___ 3. Are the results discussed in terms of the literature cited in the introduction?

Very satisfactory 5 4 3 2 1 Very unsatisfactory ***or*** N/A I/I

[5] Judge, S., & Watson, S. M. R. (2011). Longitudinal outcomes for mathematics achievement for students with learning disabilities. *The Journal of Educational Research, 104*, 147–157.

[6] Shillington, A. M., Clapp, J. D., & Reed, M. B. (2011). The stability of self-reported marijuana use across eight years of the National Longitudinal Survey of Youth. *Journal of Child & Adolescent Substance Abuse, 20*, 407–420.

Comment: The literature cited in the introduction sets the stage for the research. Thus, it is important to describe how the results of the current research relate to the literature cited at the beginning of the research report.

Researchers might address issues such as the following: Are the results consistent with those previously reported in the literature? With only some of them? With none of them? Does the study fill a gap in the literature? These are important issues to consider when drawing conclusions from a particular study. For instance, if the results of a study being evaluated are inconsistent with the results of a large number of other studies in the literature, the researcher should discuss this discrepancy and speculate on why his or her study is inconsistent with earlier ones. Examples 12.3.1 and 12.3.2 are from Discussion sections and illustrate how some researchers refer to previously cited literature.

Example 12.3.1[7]

Discussion in terms of literature mentioned in the introduction:

The present study provides results that are consistent with previous research. First, quizzes increased attendance (Azorlosa & Renner, 2006; Hovell et al., 1979; Wilder et al., 2001) and second, they increased self-reported studying (Azorlosa & Renner, 2006; Marchant, 2002; Ruscio, 2001; Wilder et al., 2001).

Example 12.3.2[8]

Discussion in terms of literature mentioned in the introduction:

The univariate findings of the present study were consistent with those of researchers (Ackerman, Brown, & Izard, 2004) who have found that family instability (i.e., cohabiting with multiple partners over a 3-year period of time) is associated with poorer outcomes for children, compared with children whose mothers get married. I did not find, however, that cohabitation with multiple partners was significantly associated with child literacy in the multivariate analyses.

___ 4. Have the researchers avoided citing new references in the Discussion section?

Very satisfactory 5 4 3 2 1 Very unsatisfactory ***or*** N/A I/I

Comment: The relevant literature should be first cited in the introduction. The literature referred to in the Discussion section should be limited to that originally cited in the introduction.

---

[7] Azorlosa, J. L. (2011). The effect of announced quizzes on exam performance: II. *Journal of Instructional Psychology*, *38*, 3–7.

[8] Fagan, J. (2011). Effect on preschoolers' literacy when never-married mothers get married. *Journal of Marriage and Family*, *73*, 1001–1014.

___ 5. Are specific implications discussed?

Very satisfactory 5 4 3 2 1 Very unsatisfactory ***or*** N/A I/I

Comment: Research often has implications for practicing professionals. When this is the case, a statement of implications should specifically describe, whenever possible, what a person, group, or institution should do on the basis of the results of the current study. Consumers of research will want to know what the researchers (who are experts on the topic) think the implications are. Example 12.5.1 is a sample statement of implications, which refers to a specific implication that might be taken (developing an anonymous reporting system).

Example 12.5.1[9]

A statement of specific implications:

Our findings demonstrate that public transportation in an urban area serves as an efficient media vehicle by which alcohol advertisers can heavily expose school-aged youths and low-income groups. In light of the health risks associated with drinking among youths and low-income populations, as well as the established link between alcohol consumption among both youths and adults, the state of Massachusetts should consider eliminating alcohol advertising on its public transit system.

Other cities and states that allow alcohol advertising on their public transit systems should also consider eliminating this advertising to protect vulnerable populations, including underage students, from potentially extensive exposure.

Example 12.5.2 also illustrates how practical implications can be drawn from research results and presented in Discussion sections.

Example 12.5.2[10]

A statement of specific implications:

The results of this study offer important implications for counselor education. We found that stereotypes related to race-ethnicity and gender do exist among individuals working toward licensure as a professional counselor. While it should be acknowledged that the existence of stereotypes does not automatically lead to discrimination against the stereotyped groups, if care is not exercised, then these stereotypes could easily guide someone's behavior and lead to discrimination. It is especially critical to avoid this in the counseling field, as clients require understanding and skillful counselors to help them when they are experiencing difficulties. Therefore, it is important that education about stereo-

---

[9] Gentry, E., Poirier, K., Wilkinson, T., Nhean, S., Nyborn, J., & Siegel, M. (2011). Alcohol advertising at Boston subway stations: An assessment of exposure by race and socioeconomic status. *American Journal of Public Health*, *101*, 1936–1941.

[10] Poyrazli, S., & Hand, D. B. (2011). Using drawings to facilitate multicultural competency development. *Journal of Instructional Psychology*, *38*, 93–104.

types and bias be consistently and thoroughly pursued in programs educating future counselors.

___ 6. Are the results discussed in terms of any relevant theories?

Very satisfactory 5 4 3 2 1 Very unsatisfactory ***or*** N/A I/I

Comment: As indicated in earlier chapters, research that tests and/or develops theories is often important because theories provide the basis for numerous predictions and implications. If a study was introduced as theory-driven (or clearly based on certain theoretical considerations), it is appropriate to describe how the current results affect interpretation of the theory in the Discussion section at the end of the research article.

Example 12.6.1 is from the beginning of a discussion of a study based on attachment theory.

Example 12.6.1[11]

Discussion section pointing out relation to theory:

The results of this study also may have important implications for the theories relating to social dominance. The strong association between competitiveness and physical, relational, and verbal aggression supports a basic premise of the theories. Competitive-aggressive dominant students do seek to establish a high place in a dominance hierarchy. However, it is perhaps only competitors that perceive a dominance hierarchy and, therefore, the theories' predictions may be limited to....

___ 7. Are suggestions for future research specific?

Very satisfactory 5 4 3 2 1 Very unsatisfactory ***or*** N/A I/I

Comment: It is uninformative for researchers to conclude with a simple phrase such as "more research is needed." To be helpful, researchers should point to specific areas and research procedures that might be fruitful in future research. This is illustrated in Example 12.7.1.

Example 12.7.1[12]

Specific suggestions for future research in a Discussion section:

[The] current study did not examine how different types of support (e.g., emotional and instrumental) may influence the relations between depression, peer victimization, and social support. Thus, future studies should examine how a

---

[11] Choi, J., Johnson, D. W., & Johnson, R. (2011). The roots of social dominance: Aggression, prosocial behavior, and social interdependence. *The Journal of Educational Research*, *104*, 442–454.

[12] Tanigawa, D., Furlong, M. J., Felix, E. D., & Sharkey, J. D. (2011). The protective role of perceived social support against the manifestation of depressive symptoms in peer victims. *Journal of School Violence*, *10*, 393–412.

combination of source and type of social support (e.g., emotional support from parents) may influence relations between stressors and outcomes.

Often, the suggestions for future research indicate how future studies can overcome the limitations in the current study. This is illustrated in Example 12.7.2.

Example 12.7.2[13]
Specific suggestions for future research in a Discussion section:
There are several limitations to this study that also suggest directions for future research. First, all measures were completed by a single reporter, with no objective verification of sleep patterns and sleep disruptions. Future studies should include an objective measure of sleep patterns (e.g., actigraphy) and maternal functioning (e.g., missed days of work due to fatigue or sleepiness). Second, whereas this study highlights the relationship between child sleep disruptions and maternal sleep and functioning, future studies should include additional family focused variables, as disrupted child sleep likely affects all members of the family. For example, parents often disagree on how to handle child night wakings, which could negatively impact marital quality. Alternatively, a mother who is fatigued due to the disrupted sleep of one child may lack the energy to effectively parent other children. Finally, this study was limited by the relatively homogeneous sample, which favored educated Caucasian women. Future studies should continue to examine how children's sleep disturbances impact sleep and functioning in a more diverse sample, as well as include fathers and siblings.

___ 8. Have the researchers distinguished between speculation and data-based conclusions?

Very satisfactory 5 4 3 2 1 Very unsatisfactory ***or*** N/A I/I

Comment: It is acceptable for researchers to speculate in the Discussion section (e.g., what the results might have been if the methodology had been different). However, it is important that researchers clearly distinguish between their speculation and the conclusions that can be justified by the data they have gathered. This can be done with some simple wording such as "It is interesting to speculate on the reasons for...."

___ 9. Overall, is the Discussion section effective and appropriate?

Very satisfactory 5 4 3 2 1 Very unsatisfactory ***or*** N/A I/I

Comment: Rate this evaluation question after considering your answers to the earlier ones in this chapter, taking into account any additional considerations and concerns you may have.

---

[13] Meltzer, L. J., & Mindell, J. A. (2007). Relationship between child sleep disturbances and maternal sleep, mood, and parenting stress: A pilot study. *Journal of Family Psychology*, *21*, 67–73.

Exercise for Chapter 12

Part A

Directions: Answer the following questions.

1. The methodological weaknesses of a study are sometimes discussed under what subheading?

2. What are the two most common types of limitations?

3. Is it ever appropriate to mention literature that was cited earlier in a research article *again* in the Discussion section at the end of a research article? Explain.

4. Suppose the entire statement of implications at the end of a research article is "Educators should pay more attention to students' needs." In your opinion, is this sufficiently specific? Explain.

5. Suppose this is the entire suggestion for future research stated at the end of a research article: "Due to the less-than-definitive nature of the current research, future research is needed on the effects of negative political campaign advertisements." In your opinion, is this sufficiently specific? Explain.

6. Is it acceptable for researchers to speculate in the Discussion section of their research reports? Explain.

Part B

Directions: Locate several research reports of interest to you in academic journals. Read them, and evaluate the Discussion sections in light of the evaluation questions in this chapter, taking into account any other considerations and concerns you may have. Select the one to which you gave the highest overall rating, and bring it to class for discussion. Be prepared to discuss its strengths and weaknesses.

Chapter 13

Putting It All Together

As a final step, a consumer of research should make an overall judgment on the quality of a research report by considering the report as a whole. The following evaluation questions are designed to help in this activity.

___ 1. In your judgment, has the researcher selected an important problem?

Very satisfactory 5 4 3 2 1 Very unsatisfactory ***or*** N/A I/I

Comment: Evaluation Question 2 in Chapter 4 asks whether the researcher has established the importance of the problem area. The evaluation question being considered here is somewhat different from the previous one because this question asks whether *the evaluator* judges the problem to be important—even if the researcher has failed to make a strong case for its importance. In such a case, a consumer of research would give the research report a high rating on this evaluation question but a low rating on Evaluation Question 2 in Chapter 4.

Note that a methodologically strong study on a trivial problem is a flaw that cannot be compensated for even with the best research methodology and report writing. On the other hand, a methodologically weak and poorly written study on an important topic may be judged to make a contribution—especially if there are no stronger studies available on the same topic.

___ 2. Were the researchers reflective?

Very satisfactory 5 4 3 2 1 Very unsatisfactory ***or*** N/A I/I

Comment: Researchers should reflect on their methodological decisions and share these reflections with their readers. This shows that careful thinking underlies their work. For instance, do they reflect on why they worked with one kind of sample rather than another? Do they discuss their reasons for selecting one measure over another for use in their research? Do they discuss their rationale for other design and procedural decisions made in designing and conducting their research?

Researchers also should reflect on their interpretations of the data. Are there other ways to interpret the data? Are the various possible interpretations described and evaluated? Do they make clear why they favor one interpretation over another?

Such reflections can appear throughout research reports and often are repeated in the Discussion section at the end.

___ 3. Is the report cohesive?

Very satisfactory 5 4 3 2 1 Very unsatisfactory ***or*** N/A I/I

Comment: Do the researchers make clear the heart of the matter (usually the research hypotheses, purposes, or questions) and write a report that revolves around it? Is the report cohesive (i.e., does it flow logically from one section to another)? Note that a scattered, incoherent report has little chance of making an important contribution to the understanding of a topic.

___ 4. Does the report extend the boundaries of the knowledge on a topic, especially for understanding relevant theories?

Very satisfactory 5 4 3 2 1 Very unsatisfactory ***or*** N/A I/I

Comment: By introducing new variables or improved methods, researchers are often able to expand understanding of a problem. It is especially helpful when their findings provide insights into various theories or provide data that may be used for theory development. When researchers believe their data clearly extend the boundaries of what is known about a research problem, they should state their reasons for this belief.

Example 13.4.1 is from the introduction to a research report. The researchers state that their research has the potential to extend the boundaries of knowledge by filling in gaps in knowledge of a topic.

Example 13.4.1[1]

Researchers state in the introduction that their study will extend knowledge by filling gaps (italics added for emphasis):

Close relationships are the setting in which some of life's most tumultuous emotions are experienced. Echoing this viewpoint, Berscheid and Reis (1998) have argued that identifying both the origins and the profile of emotions that are experienced in a relationship is essential if one wants to understand the core defining features of a relationship. Against this backdrop, one might expect that a great deal would be known about emotions in relationships, especially how significant relationship experiences at critical stages of social development forecast the type and intensity of emotions experienced in adult attachment relationships. Surprisingly little is known about these issues, however (see Berscheid & Regan, 2004; Shaver, Morgan, & Wu, 1996). *Using attachment theory (Bowlby, 1969, 1973, 1980) as an organizing framework, we designed the current longitudinal study to fill these crucial conceptual and empirical gaps in our knowledge.*

---

[1] Simpson, J. A., Collins, W. A., Tran, S., & Haydon, K. C. (2007). Attachment and the experience and expression of emotions in romantic relationships: A developmental perspective. *Journal of Personality and Social Psychology*, *92*, 355–367.

Example 13.4.2 is excerpted from the Discussion section of a research report in which the researchers explicitly state that their findings replicate and extend what is known about an issue.

Example 13.4.2[2]

Researchers state in the Discussion section that their study extended knowledge of the topic (bold italics added for emphasis):

The present study extends beyond prior descriptions of interventions for homeless families by providing detailed information about a comprehensive health center-based intervention. Findings demonstrate that it is feasible to integrate services that address the physical and behavioral health and support needs of homeless families in a primary health care setting. Detailed descriptive data presented about staff roles and activities begin to establish parameters for fidelity assessment, an essential first step to ensure adequate replication and rigorous testing of the HFP model in other settings.

Example 13.4.3 is excerpted from the Discussion section of a research report in which the researchers note that their results provide support for a theory.

Example 13.4.3[3]

Researchers state in the Discussion section that their study helps to support a theory (bold italics added for emphasis):

Study 1 provided evidence in support of the first proposition of a new dialect theory of communicating emotion. As in previous studies of spontaneous expressions (Camras, Oster, Campos, Miyake, & Bradshaw, 1997; Ekman, 1972), posed emotional expressions converged greatly across cultural groups, in support of basic universality. However, reliable cultural differences also emerged. Thus, the study provided direct empirical support for a central proposition of dialect theory, to date supported only by indirect evidence from emotion recognition studies (e.g., Elfenbein & Ambady, 2002b). Differences were not merely idiosyncratic to....

___ 5. Are any major methodological flaws unavoidable or forgivable?

Very satisfactory 5 4 3 2 1 Very unsatisfactory ***or*** N/A I/I

Comment: No study is perfect, but some are more seriously flawed than others. When serious flaws are encountered, consider whether they were unavoidable. For instance, obtaining a random sample of street prostitutes for a study on AIDS transmission is probably impossible. However, if the researchers went to considerable effort to contact

---

[2] Weinreb, L., Nicholson, J., Williams, V., & Anthes, F. (2007). Integrating behavioral health services for homeless mothers and children in primary care. *American Journal of Orthopsychiatry*, *77*, 142–152.

[3] Elfenbein, H. A., Beaupré, M., Lévesque, M., & Hess, U. (2007). Toward a dialect theory: Cultural differences in the expression and recognition of posed facial expressions. *Emotion*, *7*, 131–146.

potential participants at different times of the day in various locations (not just the safer parts of a city) and obtained a high rate of participation from those who were contacted, the failure to obtain a random sample would be forgivable because the flaw was unavoidable and considerable effort was made to overcome the flaw.

Contrast the preceding example with a study in which researchers want to generalize from a sample of fourth graders to a larger population but simply settle for a classroom of students who are readily accessible because they attend the university's demonstration school on the university campus. The failure to use random sampling, or at least to use a more diverse sample from various classrooms, is not unavoidable and should be counted as a flaw.

Unless some flaws under some circumstances are tolerated, the vast majority of research in the social and behavioral sciences would need to be summarily rejected. Instead, as a practical matter, consumers of research tolerate certain flaws but interpret the data from seriously flawed studies with considerable caution.

___ 6. Is the research likely to inspire additional research?

Very satisfactory 5 4 3 2 1 Very unsatisfactory ***or*** N/A I/I

Comment: Even if a study is seriously flawed, it can receive a high evaluation on this question if it is likely to inspire others to study the problem. Seriously flawed research is most likely to get high ratings on this evaluation question if it employs novel research methods, has surprising findings, or helps to advance the development of a theory. Keep in mind that research on a problem is an ongoing *process*, with each study contributing to the base of knowledge about a topic. A study that stimulates the process and moves it forward is worthy of attention—even if it is seriously flawed or is only a pilot study.

___ 7. Is the research likely to help in decision making?

Very satisfactory 5 4 3 2 1 Very unsatisfactory ***or*** N/A I/I

Comment: Even seriously flawed research sometimes can help decision makers. Suppose a researcher conducted an experiment on a new drug-resistance educational program with no control group (usually considered a serious flaw) and found that students' illicit drug usage actually went up from pretest to posttest. Such a finding might lead to the decision to abandon the educational program, especially if other studies with different types of flaws produced results consistent with this one.

When applying this evaluation question, consider the following: In the absence of any other studies on the same topic, would this study help decision makers arrive at more informed decisions than they would if the study did not exist?

___ 8. All things considered, is the report worthy of publication in an academic journal?

Very satisfactory 5 4 3 2 1 Very unsatisfactory ***or*** N/A I/I

Comment: Given that space is limited in academic journals, with some journals rejecting more than 90% of the research reports submitted, is the report being evaluated worthy of publication?

___ 9. Would you be proud to have your name on the research article as a co-author?

Very satisfactory 5 4 3 2 1 Very unsatisfactory ***or*** N/A I/I

Comment: This is the most subjective evaluation question in this book, and it is fitting that it is last. Would you want to be personally associated with the research you are evaluating?

Concluding Comment

I hope that as a result of reading and working through this book, you have become a critical consumer of research while recognizing that conducting solid research in the social and behavioral sciences is often difficult (and conducting "perfect research" is impossible).

Note that the typical research methods textbook attempts to show *what should be done in the ideal*. Textbook authors do this because their usual purpose is to train students in how to conduct research. Unless a student knows what the ideal standards for research are, he or she is likely to fall unintentionally into many traps.

However, when evaluating reports of research in academic journals, it is unreasonable to hold each research article up to ideal "textbook standards." Researchers conduct research under less-than-ideal conditions, usually with limited resources. In addition, they typically are forced to make many compromises (especially in measurement and sampling) given the practical realities of typical research settings. A fair and meaningful evaluation of a research article takes these practical matters into consideration.

Notes

Appendix A

Quantitative and Qualitative Research: An Overview[1]

Because *quantitative* researchers reduce information to statistics such as averages, percentages, and so on, their research reports are easy to spot. If a report has a Results section devoted mainly to the presentation of statistical data, it is a report of quantitative research. This approach to research dominated the social and behavioral sciences throughout most of the 1900s and still represents the majority of published research in the 2000s. Thus, for most topics, you are likely to locate many more articles reporting quantitative research than qualitative research.

In the ideal, those who conduct *quantitative research* should do the following:

1. Start with one or more very specific, explicitly stated research hypotheses, purposes, or questions, ideally derived from theory and/or previous research. Make research plans that focus narrowly on the stated hypotheses, purposes, or questions (as opposed to being wide-ranging and exploratory).
2. Select a random sample (like drawing names out of a hat) from a population so that the sample is representative of the population from which it was drawn.[2]
3. Use a relatively large sample of participants, sometimes as many as 1,500 for a national survey. Some quantitative researchers use even larger samples, but many use much smaller ones because of limited resources. A study with a large sample is usually a quantitative one.
4. Make observations with measures that can be scored objectively, such as multiple-choice achievement tests and attitude scales in which participants mark choices such as "strongly agree" and "strongly disagree."
5. Describe results using statistics, and make inferences to the population from which the sample was drawn (i.e., inferring that what the researcher found by studying a sample is similar to what he or she would have found by studying the entire population from which the sample was drawn).

In addition, quantitative research is characterized by "distance" between researchers and their participants. That is, quantitative researchers typically have limited contact

---

[1] This appendix is based in part on material drawn with permission from Galvan, J. L. (2009). *Writing literature reviews: A guide for students of the social and behavioral sciences* (4th ed.). Glendale, CA: Pyrczak Publishing.

[2] It is representative except for the effects of random errors, which can be assessed with inferential statistics. Chapter 7 points out that researchers do not always sample or need random samples.

with their participants. In fact, it is not uncommon for the researcher to have no direct contact with them. For instance, a quantitative researcher might have teachers administer tests to students without ever seeing or talking with the students. Even if the researcher is physically present in the research setting, he or she usually follows a prearranged script for the study and avoids unplanned personal interactions.

Qualitative research also has a long tradition in the social and behavioral sciences, but it has gained a large following in many applied fields only in recent decades. It is also often easy to identify because the titles of the articles frequently contain the word *qualitative*. In addition, qualitative researchers usually identify their research as qualitative in their Introductions as well as in other parts of their reports.[3] You can also identify qualitative research because the Results section will be presented in a narrative describing themes and trends, which are very often illustrated with quotations from the participants.

In the ideal, those who conduct *qualitative research* should do the following:

1. Start with a general research question or problem, and *not* formulate hypotheses derived from previously published literature or theories. Although qualitative researchers avoid starting with hypotheses and theories, they may emerge while the research is being conducted (i.e., a qualitative researcher may formulate hypotheses or theories that explain his or her observations). Such hypotheses and theories are subject to change as additional data are collected during the study. Thus, there is a fluid interaction between the data collection, data analysis, and any hypotheses or theories that may emerge.
2. Select a purposive sample—not a random one. A purposive sample is one in which the researcher has some special research interest and is not necessarily representative of a larger population. In other words, the researcher intentionally draws what he or she believes to be an appropriate sample for the research problem, without regard to random selection.
3. Use a relatively small sample—sometimes as small as one exemplary case, but more often small groups of people or units such as classrooms, churches, and so on.
4. Observe with relatively unstructured measures such as semistructured interviews, unstructured direct observations, and so on.
5. Observe intensively (e.g., spending extended periods of time with the participants to gain in-depth insights into the phenomena of interest).
6. Present results mainly or exclusively in words, with an emphasis on understanding the particular purposive sample studied and a de-emphasis on making generalizations to larger populations.

In addition, qualitative research is characterized by the researchers' awareness of their own orientations, biases, and experiences that might affect their collection and in-

[3] Note that quantitative researchers rarely explicitly state that their research is quantitative. Because the overwhelming majority of research reports in journals are quantitative, readers will assume that it is quantitative unless told otherwise.

terpretation of data. It is not uncommon for qualitative researchers to include in their research reports a statement on these issues and what steps they took to see beyond their own subjective experiences in order to understand their research problems from the participants' points of view. Thus, there is a tendency for qualitative research to be personal and interactive. This is in contrast to quantitative research, in which researchers attempt to be objective and distant.

As can be seen in this appendix, the fact that the two research traditions are quite distinct must be taken into account when research reports are being evaluated. Those who are just beginning to learn about qualitative research are urged to read Appendix B in this book, which discusses some important issues in its evaluation.

Notes

Appendix B

Examining the Validity Structure of Qualitative Research

R. BURKE JOHNSON
University of South Alabama

ABSTRACT. Three types of validity in qualitative research are discussed. First, descriptive validity refers to the factual accuracy of the account as reported by the qualitative researcher. Second, interpretive validity is obtained to the degree that the participants' viewpoints, thoughts, intentions, and experiences are accurately understood and reported by the qualitative researcher. Third, theoretical validity is obtained to the degree that a theory or theoretical explanation developed from a research study fits the data and is, therefore, credible and defensible. The two types of validity that are typical of quantitative research, internal and external validity, are also discussed for qualitative research. Thirteen strategies used to promote research validity in qualitative research are discussed.

Discussions of the term "validity" have traditionally been attached to the quantitative research tradition. Not surprisingly, reactions by qualitative researchers have been mixed regarding whether or not this concept should be applied to qualitative research. At the extreme, some qualitative researchers have suggested that the traditional quantitative criteria of reliability and validity are not relevant to qualitative research (e.g., Smith, 1984). Smith contends that the basic epistemological and ontological assumptions of quantitative and qualitative research are incompatible, and, therefore, the concepts of reliability and validity should be abandoned. Most qualitative researchers, however, probably hold a more moderate viewpoint. Most qualitative researchers argue that some qualitative research studies are better than others, and they frequently use the term validity to refer to this difference. When qualitative researchers speak of research validity, they are usually referring to qualitative research that is plausible, credible, trustworthy, and, therefore, defensible. We believe it is important to think about the issue of validity in qualitative research and to examine some strategies that have been developed to maximize validity (Kirk & Miller, 1986; LeCompte & Preissle, 1993; Lincoln & Guba, 1985; Maxwell, 1996). A list of these strategies is provided in Table 1.

One potential threat to validity that researchers must be careful to watch out for is called *researcher bias.* This problem is summed up in a statement a colleague of mine once made to me. She said, "The problem with qualitative research is that the researchers find what they want to find, and then they write up their results." It is true that the problem of researcher bias is frequently an issue because qualitative research is open-ended and less structured than quantitative research. This is because qualitative research tends to be exploratory. (One would be remiss, however, to think that researcher bias is never a problem in quantitative research.) Researcher bias tends to result from selective observation and selective recording of information, and also from allowing one's personal views and perspectives to affect how data are interpreted and how the research is conducted.

The key strategy used to understand researcher bias is called *reflexivity,* which means that the researcher actively engages in critical self-reflection about his or her potential biases and predispositions (Table 1). Through reflexivity, researchers become more self-aware, and they monitor and attempt to control their biases. Many qualitative

Table 1
Strategies Used to Promote Qualitative Research Validity

Strategy	Description
Researcher as "detective"	A metaphor characterizing the qualitative researcher as he or she searches for evidence about causes and effects. The researcher develops an understanding of the data through careful consideration of potential causes and effects and by systematically eliminating "rival" explanations or hypotheses until the final "case" is made "beyond a reasonable doubt." The "detective" can utilize any of the strategies listed here.
Extended fieldwork	When possible, qualitative researchers should collect data in the field over an extended period of time.
Low inference descriptors	The use of description phrased very close to the participants' accounts and researchers' field notes. Verbatims (i.e., direct quotations) are a commonly used type of low inference descriptors.
Triangulation	"Cross-checking" information and conclusions through the use of multiple procedures or sources. When the different procedures or sources are in agreement, you have "corroboration."
Data triangulation	The use of multiple data sources to help understand a phenomenon.
Methods triangulation	The use of multiple research methods to study a phenomenon.
Investigator triangulation	The use of multiple investigators (i.e., multiple researchers) in collecting and interpreting the data.
Theory triangulation	The use of multiple theories and perspectives to help interpret and explain the data.
Participant feedback	The feedback and discussion of the researcher's interpretations and conclusions with the actual participants and other members of the participant community for verification and insight.
Peer review	Discussion of the researcher's interpretations and conclusions with other people. This includes discussion with a "disinterested peer" (e.g., with another researcher not directly involved). This peer should be skeptical and play the "devil's advocate," challenging the researcher to provide solid evidence for any interpretations or conclusions. Discussion with peers who are familiar with the research can also help provide useful challenges and insights.
Negative case sampling	Locating and examining cases that disconfirm the researcher's expectations and tentative explanation.
Reflexivity	This involves self-awareness and "critical self-reflection" by the researcher on his or her potential biases and predispositions as these may affect the research process and conclusions.
Pattern matching	Predicting a series of results that form a "pattern" and then determining the degree to which the actual results fit the predicted pattern.

researchers include a distinct section in their research proposals titled Researcher Bias. In this section, they discuss their personal background, how it may affect their research, and what strategies they will use to address the potential problem. Another strategy that qualitative researchers use to reduce the effect of researcher bias is called *negative case sampling* (Table 1). This means that they attempt carefully and purposively to search for examples that disconfirm their expectations and explanations about what they are studying. If you use this approach, you will find it more difficult to ignore important information, and you will come up with more credible and defensible results.

We will now examine some types of validity that are important in qualitative research. We will start with three types of validity that are especially relevant to qualitative research (Maxwell, 1992, 1996). These types are called descriptive validity, interpretive validity, and theoretical validity. They are important to qualitative research because description of what is observed and interpretation of participants' thoughts are two primary qualitative research activities. For example, ethnography produces descriptions and accounts of the lives and experiences of groups of people with a focus on cultural characteristics (Fetterman, 1998; LeCompte & Preissle, 1993). Ethnographers also attempt to understand groups of people from the insider's perspective (i.e., from the viewpoints of the people in the group; called the *emic* perspective). Developing a theoretical explanation of the behavior of group members is also of interest to qualitative researchers, especially qualitative researchers using the grounded theory perspective (Glaser & Strauss, 1967; Strauss & Corbin, 1990). After discussing these three forms of validity, the traditional types of validity used in quantitative research, internal and external validity, are discussed. Internal validity is relevant when qualitative researchers explore cause and effect relationships. External validity is relevant when qualitative researchers generalize beyond their research studies.

Descriptive Validity

The first type of validity in qualitative research is called *descriptive validity.* Descriptive validity refers to the factual accuracy of the account as reported by the researchers. The key questions addressed in descriptive validity are: Did what was reported as taking place in the group being studied actually happen? and Did the researchers accurately report what they saw and heard? In other words, descriptive validity refers to accuracy in reporting descriptive information (e.g., description of events, objects, behaviors, people, settings, times, and places). This form of validity is important because description is a major objective in nearly all qualitative research.

One effective strategy used to obtain descriptive validity is called *investigator triangulation.* In the case of descriptive validity, investigator triangulation involves the use of multiple observers to record and describe the research participants' behavior and the context in which they were located. The use of multiple observers allows cross-checking of observations to make sure the investigators agree about what took place. When corroboration (i.e., agreement) of observations across multiple investigators is obtained, it is less likely that outside reviewers of the research will question whether something occurred. As a result, the research will be more credible and defensible.

Interpretive Validity

While descriptive validity refers to accuracy in reporting the facts, interpretive validity requires developing a window into the minds of the people being studied. *Interpretive validity* refers to accurately portraying the *meaning* attached by participants to what is being studied by the researcher. More specifically, it refers to the degree to which the research participants' viewpoints, thoughts, feelings, intentions, and experiences are accurately understood by the qualitative researcher and portrayed in the research report. An important part of qualitative research is understanding research participants' inner worlds (i.e., their phenomenological worlds), and interpretive validity refers to the degree of accuracy in presenting these inner worlds. Accurate interpretive validity requires that the researcher gets inside the heads of the participants, looks through the participants' eyes, and sees and feels what they see and feel. In this way, the qualitative researcher can understand things from the participants' perspectives and provide a valid account of these perspectives.

Some strategies for achieving interpretive validity are provided in Table 1. *Participant feedback* is perhaps the most important strategy (Table 1). This strategy has also been called "member checking" (Lincoln & Guba, 1985). By sharing your interpretations of participants' viewpoints with the participants and other members of the group, you may clear up areas of miscommunication. Do the people being studied agree with what you have said about them? While this strategy is not perfect because some participants may attempt to put on a good face, useful information is frequently obtained and inaccuracies are often identified.

When writing the research report, using many *low inference descriptors* is also helpful so that the reader can experience the participants' actual language, dialect, and personal meanings (Table 1). A verbatim is the lowest inference descriptor of all because the participants' exact words are provided in direct quotations. Here is an example of a verbatim from a high school dropout who was part of an ethnographic study of high school dropouts:

> I wouldn't do the work. I didn't like the teacher and I didn't like my mom and dad. So, even if I did my work, I wouldn't turn it in. I completed it. I just didn't want to turn it in. I was angry with my mom and dad because they were talking about moving out of state at the time (Okey & Cusick, 1995: p. 257).

This verbatim provides some description (i.e., what the participant did) but it also provides some information about the participant's interpretations and personal meanings (which is the topic of interpretive validity). The participant expresses his frustration and anger toward his parents and teacher, and shares with us what homework meant to him at the time and why he acted as he did. By reading verbatims like this one, readers of a report can experience for themselves the participants' perspectives. Again, getting into the minds of research participants is a common goal in qualitative research, and Maxwell calls our accuracy in portraying this inner content interpretive validity.

Theoretical Validity

The third type of validity in qualitative research is called *theoretical validity.* You have theoretical validity to the degree that a theoretical explanation developed from a research study fits the data and, therefore, is credible and defensible. Theory usually refers to discussions of *how* a phenomenon operates and *why* it operates as it does. Theory is usually more abstract and less concrete than description and interpretation. Theory development moves beyond just the facts and provides an explanation of the phenomenon. In the words of Joseph Maxwell (1992):

> One could label the student's throwing of the eraser as an act of resistance, and connect this act to the repressive behavior or values of the teacher, the social structure of the school, and class relationships in U.S. society. The identification of the throwing as resistance constitutes the application of a theoretical construct...the connection of this to other aspects of the participants, the school, or the community constitutes the postulation of theoretical relationships among these constructs (p. 291).

In the above example, the theoretical construct called "resistance" is used to explain the student's behavior. Maxwell points out that the construct of resistance may also be related to other theoretical constructs or variables. In fact, theories are often developed by relating theoretical constructs.

A strategy for promoting theoretical validity is *extended fieldwork* (Table 1). This means that you should spend a sufficient amount of time studying your research participants and their setting so that you can have confidence that the patterns of relationships you believe are operating are stable and so that you can understand why these relationships occur. As you spend more time in the field collecting data and generating and testing your inductive hypotheses, your theoretical explanation may become more detailed and intricate. You may also decide to use the strategy called *theory triangulation* (Table 1). This means that you would examine how the phenomenon being studied would be explained by different theories. The various theories might provide you with insights and help you develop a more cogent explanation. In a related way, you might also use investigator triangulation and consider the ideas and explanations generated by additional researchers studying the research participants.

As you develop your theoretical explanation, you should make some predictions based on the theory and test the accuracy of those predictions. When doing this, you can use the *pattern matching* strategy (Table 1). In pattern matching, the strategy is to make several predictions at once; then, if all of the predictions occur as predicted (i.e., if the pattern is found), you have evidence supporting your explanation. As you develop your theoretical explanation, you should also use the *negative case sampling* strategy mentioned earlier (Table 1). That is, you must always search for cases or examples that do not fit your explanation so that you do not simply find the data that support your developing theory. As a general rule, your final explanation should accurately reflect the majority of the people in your research study. Another useful strategy for promoting theoretical validity is called *peer review* (Table 1). This means that you should try to spend some time discussing your explanation with your colleagues so that they can search for problems with it. Each problem must then be resolved. In some cases, you will find that you will need to go back to the field and collect additional data. Finally, when developing a theoretical explanation, you must also think about the issues of internal validity and external validity, to which we now turn.

Internal Validity

Internal validity is the fourth type of validity in qualitative research of interest to us. Internal validity refers to the degree to which a researcher is justified in concluding that an observed relationship is causal (Cook & Campbell, 1979). Often, qualitative researchers are not interested in cause-and-effect relationships. Sometimes, however, qualitative researchers are interested in identifying potential causes and effects. In fact, qualitative research can be very helpful in describing how phenomena operate (i.e., studying process) and in developing and testing preliminary causal hypotheses and theories (Campbell, 1979; Johnson, 1994; LeCompte & Preissle, 1993; Strauss, 1995; 1994).

When qualitative researchers identify potential cause-and-effect relationships, they must think about many of the same issues that quantitative researchers must consider. They should also think about the strategies used for obtaining theoretical validity discussed earlier. The qualitative researcher takes on the role of the detective searching for the true cause(s) of a phenomenon, examining each possible clue, and attempting to rule out each rival explanation generated (see *Researcher as "detective"* in Table 1). When trying to identify a causal relationship, the researcher makes mental comparisons. The comparison might be to a hypothetical control group. Although a control group is rarely used in qualitative research, the researcher can think about what would have happened if the causal factor had not occurred. The researcher can sometimes rely on his or her expert opinion, as well as published research studies when available, in deciding what would have happened. Furthermore, if the event is something that occurs again, the researcher can determine if the causal factor precedes the outcome. In other words, when the causal factor occurs again, does the effect follow?

When a researcher believes that an observed relationship is causal, he or she must also attempt to make sure that the observed change in the dependent variable is due to the independent variable and not to something else (e.g., a confounding extraneous variable). The successful researcher will always make a list of rival explanations or rival hypotheses, which are possible or plausible reasons for the relationship other than the originally suspected cause. Be creative and think of as many rival explanations as you can. One way to get started is to be a skeptic and think of reasons why the relationship should not be causal. Each rival explanation must be examined after the list has been developed. Sometimes you will be able to check a rival explanation with the data you have already collected through additional data analysis. At other times you will need to collect additional data. One strategy would be to observe the relationship you believe to be causal under conditions where the confounding variable is not present and compare this outcome with the original outcome. For example, if you concluded that a teacher effectively maintained classroom discipline on a given day but a critic maintained that it was the result of a parent visiting the classroom on that day, then you should try to observe the teacher again when the parent is not present. If the teacher is still successful, you have some evidence that the original finding was not because of the presence of the parent in the classroom.

All of the strategies shown in Table 1 are used to improve the internal validity of qualitative research. Now we will explain the only two strategies not yet discussed (i.e., methods triangulation and data triangulation). When using *methods triangulation*, the researcher uses more than one method of research in a single research study. The word "methods" should be used broadly here, and it refers to different methods of research (e.g., ethnography, survey, experimental, etc.) as well as to different types of data collection procedures (e.g., interviews, questionnaires, and observations). You can intermix any of these (e.g., ethnography and survey research methods, or interviews and observations, or experimental research and interviews). The logic is to combine different methods that have "nonoverlapping weaknesses and strengths" (Brewer & Hunter, 1989). The weaknesses (and strengths) of one method will tend to be different from those of a different method, which means that when you combine two or more methods, you will have better evidence! In other words, the "whole" is better than its "parts."

Here is an example of methods triangulation. Perhaps you are interested in why students in an elementary classroom stigmatize a certain student named Brian. A stigmatized student would be an individual that is not well liked, has a lower status, and is seen as different from the normal students. Perhaps Brian has a different haircut from the other students, is dressed differently, or doesn't act like the other students. In this case, you might decide to observe how students treat Brian in various situations. In addition to observing the students, you will probably decide to interview Brian and the other students to understand their beliefs and feelings about Brian. A strength of observational data is that you can actually see the students' behaviors. A weakness of interviews is that what the students say and what they actually do may be different. However, using interviews you can delve into the students' thinking and reasoning, whereas you cannot do this using observational data. Therefore, the whole will likely be better than the parts.

When using *data triangulation*, the researcher uses multiple data sources in a single research study. "Data sources" does not mean using different methods. Data triangulation refers to the use of multiple data sources using a single method. For example, the use of multiple interviews would provide multiple data sources while using a single method (i.e., the interview method). Likewise, the use of multiple observations would be another example of data triangulation; multiple data sources would be provided while using a single method (i.e., the observational method). Another important part of data triangulation involves collecting data at different times, at different places, and with different people.

Here is an example of data triangulation. Perhaps a researcher is interested in studying why certain students are apathetic. It would make sense to get the perspectives of several different kinds of people. The researcher might interview teachers, interview students identified by the teachers as being apathetic, and interview peers of apathetic students. Then the researcher could check to see if the information obtained from these different data sources was in agreement. Each data source may provide additional reasons as well as a different perspective on the question of student apathy, resulting in a more complete understanding of the phenomenon. The researcher should also interview apathetic students at different class periods during the day and in different types of classes (e.g., math and social studies). Through the rich information gathered (e.g., from different people, at different times, and at different places) the researcher can develop a better understanding of why students are apathetic than if only one data source is used.

External Validity

External validity is important when you want to generalize from a set of research findings to other people, settings, and times (Cook & Campbell, 1979). Typically, generalizability is not the major purpose of qualitative research. There are at least two reasons for this. First, the people and settings examined in qualitative research are rarely randomly selected, and, as you know, random selection is the best way to generalize from a sample to a population. As a result, qualitative research is virtually always weak in the form of population validity focused on "generalizing to populations" (i.e., generalizing from a sample to a population).

Second, some qualitative researchers are more interested in documenting particularistic findings than universalistic findings. In other words, in certain forms of qualitative research the goal is to show what is unique about a certain group of people, or a certain event, rather than generate findings that are broadly applicable. At a fundamental level, many qualitative researchers do not believe in the presence of general laws or universal laws. General laws are things that apply to many people, and universal laws are things that apply to everyone. As a result, qualitative research is frequently considered weak on the "generalizing across populations" form of population validity (i.e., generalizing to different kinds of people), and on ecological validity (i.e., generalizing across settings) and temporal validity (i.e., generalizing across times).

Other experts argue that rough generalizations can be made from qualitative research. Perhaps the most reasonable stance toward the issue of generalizing is that we can generalize to other people, settings, and times to the degree that they are similar to the people, settings, and times in the original study. Stake (1990) uses the term *naturalistic generalization*[1] to refer to this process of generalizing based on similarity. The bottom line is this: The more similar the people and circumstances in a particular research study are to the ones that you want to generalize to, the more defensible your generalization will be and the more readily you should make such a generalization.

To help readers of a research report know when they can generalize, qualitative researchers should provide the following kinds of information: the number and kinds of people in the study, how they were selected to be in the study, contextual information, the nature of the researcher's relationship with the participants, information about any informants who provided information, the methods of data collection used, and the data analysis techniques used. This information is usually reported in the Methodology section of the final research report. Using the information included in a well-written Methodology section, readers will be able to make informed decisions about to whom the results may be generalized. They will also have the information they will need if they decide to replicate the research study with new participants.

Some experts show another way to generalize

[1] Donald Campbell (1986) makes a similar point, and he uses the term *proximal similarity* to refer to the degree of similarity between the people and circumstances in the original research study and the people and circumstances to which you wish to apply the findings. Using Campbell's term, your goal is to check for proximal similarity.

from qualitative research (e.g., Yin, 1994). Qualitative researchers can sometimes use *replication logic,* just like the replication logic that is commonly used by experimental researchers when they generalize beyond the people in their studies, even when they do not have random samples. According to replication logic, the more times a research finding is shown to be true with different sets of people, the more confidence we can place in the finding and in the conclusion that the finding generalizes beyond the people in the original research study (Cook & Campbell, 1979). In other words, if the finding is replicated with different kinds of people and in different places, then the evidence may suggest that the finding applies very broadly. Yin's key point is that there is no reason why replication logic cannot be applied to certain kinds of qualitative research.[2]

Here is an example. Over the years, you may observe a certain pattern of relations between boys and girls in your third-grade classroom. Now assume that you decided to conduct a qualitative research study and you find that the pattern of relations occurred in your classroom and in two other third-grade classrooms you studied. Because your research is interesting, you decide to publish it. Then other researchers replicate your study with other people and they find that the same relationship holds in the third-grade classrooms they studied. According to replication logic, the more times a theory or a research finding is replicated with other people, the greater the support for the theory or research finding. Now assume further that other researchers find that the relationship holds in classrooms at several other grade levels (e.g., first grade, second grade, fourth grade, and fifth grade). If this happens, the evidence suggests that the finding generalizes to students in other grade levels, adding additional generality to the finding.

One more comment before concluding: If generalizing through replication and theoretical validity (discussed above) sound similar, that is because they are. Basically, generalizing (i.e., external validity) is frequently part of theoretical validity. In other words, when researchers develop theoretical explanations, they often want to generalize beyond their original research study. Likewise, internal validity is also important for theoretical validity if cause-and-effect statements are made.

[2] The late Donald Campbell, perhaps the most important quantitative research methodologist over the past 60 years, approved of Yin's (1994) book. See, for example, his Introduction to that book.

References

Brewer, J., & Hunter, A. (1989). *Multimethod research: A synthesis of styles*. Newbury Park, CA: Sage.

Campbell, D. T. (1979). Degrees of freedom and the case study. In T. D. Cook & C. S. Reichardt (Eds.), *Qualitative and quantitative methods in evaluation research* (pp. 49–67). Beverly Hills, CA: Sage Publications.

Campbell, D. T. (1986). Relabeling internal and external validity for applied social scientists. In W. Trochim (Ed.), *Advances in quasi-experimental design and analysis: New directions for program evaluation, 31*, San Francisco: Jossey-Bass.

Cook, T. D., & Campbell, D. T. (1979). *Quasi-experimentation: Design and analysis issues for field settings*. Chicago: Rand McNally.

Denzin, N. K. (1989). *The research act: Theoretical introduction to sociological methods*. Englewood Cliffs, NJ: Prentice Hall.

Fetterman, D. M. (1998). Ethnography. In *Handbook of applied social research methods* by L. Bickman & D. J. Rog (Eds.). Thousand Oaks, CA: Sage.

Glaser, B. G., & Strauss, A. L. (1967). *The discovery of grounded theory: Strategies for qualitative research*. New York: Aldine de Gruyter.

Johnson, R. B. (1994). Qualitative research in education. *SRATE Journal, 4*(1), 3–7.

Kirk, J., & Miller, M. L. (1986). *Reliability and validity in qualitative research*. Newbury Park, CA: Sage.

LeCompte, M. D., & Preissle, J. (1993). *Ethnography and qualitative design in educational research*. San Diego, CA: Academic Press.

Lincoln, Y. S., & Guba, E. G. (1985). *Naturalistic inquiry*. Beverly Hills, CA: Sage.

Maxwell, J. A. (1992). Understanding and validity in qualitative research. *Harvard Educational Review, 62*(3), 279–299.

Maxwell, J. A. (1996). *Qualitative research design*. Newbury Park, CA: Sage.

Okey, T. N., & Cusick, P. A. (1995). Dropping out: Another side of the story. *Educational Administration Quarterly, 31*(2), 244–267.

Smith, J. K. (1984). The problem of criteria for judging interpretive inquiry. *Educational Evaluation and Policy Analysis, 6*, 379–391.

Stake, R. E. (1990). Situational context as influence on evaluation design and use. *Studies in Educational Evaluation, 16*, 231–246.

Strauss, A. (1995). Notes on the nature and development of general theories. *Qualitative Inquiry 1*(1), 7–18.

Strauss, A., & Corbin, J. (1990). *Basics of qualitative research: Grounded theory procedures and techniques*. Newbury Park, CA: Sage.

Yin, R. K. (1994). *Case study research: Design and methods*. Newbury Park, CA: Sage.

Notes

Appendix C

The Limitations of Significance Testing

Most of the quantitative research you evaluate will contain significance tests. They are important tools for quantitative researchers but have two major limitations. Before discussing the limitations, consider the purpose of significance testing and the types of information it provides.

The Function of Significance Testing

The function of significance testing is to help researchers evaluate the role of chance errors due to sampling. Statisticians refer to these chance errors as *sampling errors*. As you will see later in this appendix, it is very important to note that the term *sampling errors* is a statistical term that refers only to *chance* errors. Where do these sampling errors come from? They result from random sampling. Random sampling (e.g., drawing names out of a hat) gives everyone in a population an equal chance of being selected. Random sampling also produces random errors (once again, known as *sampling errors*). Consider Example C.1 and Example C.2 to get a better understanding of this problem. Note in Example C.1 that when whole populations are tested, there are no sampling errors and, hence, significance tests are not needed. It is also important to note that *a real difference can be a small difference* (in this example, less than a full point on a 30-item test).

Example C.1
Example with no sampling errors because a whole population of tenth graders was tested:

A team of researchers tested all 500 tenth graders in a school district with a highly reliable and valid current events test consisting of 30 multiple-choice items. The team obtained a mean (the most popular average) of 15.9 for the girls and a mean of 15.1 for the boys. In this case, the 0.8-point difference in favor of the girls is "real" because *all* boys and girls were tested. The research team did not need to conduct a significance test to help them determine whether the 0.8-point difference was due to studying just a random sample of girls, which might not be representative of all girls, and a random sample of boys, which might not be representative of all boys. (Remember that the function of significance testing is to help researchers evaluate the role of chance errors due to sampling.)

Example C.2

Example of sampling errors when there is no difference between groups:

A different team of researchers conducted the same study with the same test at about the same time as the research team in Example C.1. (They did not know the other team was conducting a population study.) This second team drew a random sample of 30 10th-grade girls and 30 10th-grade boys and obtained a mean of 16.2 for the girls and a mean of 14.9 for the boys. Why didn't they obtain the same values as the first research team? Obviously, it is because this research team sampled. Hence, the difference in results between the two studies is due to the *sampling errors* in this study.

In practice, typically only one study is conducted using random samples. If researchers are comparing the means for two groups, there will almost always be at least a small difference (and sometimes a large difference). In either case, it is conventional for quantitative researchers to conduct a significance test, which yields a probability that the difference between the means is due to sampling errors. If there is a low probability that sampling errors created the difference (such as less than 5 out of 100, or $p < .05$), then the researchers will conclude that the difference is due to something other than chance. Such a difference is called a *statistically significant difference*.

The Limitations of Significance Testing

There are three major limitations to significance testing. Without knowing them, those who conduct and evaluate the results of quantitative research are likely to be misled.

First, *a significant difference can be large or small.* While it is true that larger differences tend to be statistically significant, significance tests are built on a combination of factors that can offset each other.[1] Under certain common circumstances, small differences are statistically significant. Therefore, the first limitation of significance testing is that it does not tell us whether a difference (or relationship) is large or small. (Remember that small differences can be "real" [see Example C.1], and these can be detected by significance tests.) The obvious implication for those who are evaluating research reports is that they need to consider the magnitude of any significant differences that are reported. For instance, for the difference between two means, ask "By *how many points* do the two groups differ?" and "Is this a large difference?"

The second limitation of significance testing is that a significance test does not indicate whether the result is of practical significance. For instance, a school district might have to spend millions of dollars to purchase computer-assisted instructional software to get a statistically significant improvement (which might be indicated by a research re-

---

[1] If the difference between two means is being tested for statistical significance, three factors are combined mathematically to determine the probability: the size of the difference, the size of the sample, and the amount of variation within each group. One or two of these factors can offset the other(s). For this reason, sometimes small differences are statistically significant, and sometimes large differences are *not* statistically significant.

port). If there are tight budgetary limits, the results of the research would be of no practical significance to the district. When considering practical significance, the most common criteria are as follows: (a) cost in relation to benefit of a statistically significant improvement (e.g., how many points of improvement in mathematics achievement can we expect for each dollar spent?); (b) the political acceptability of an action based on a statistically significant research result (e.g., will local politicians and groups that influence them, such as parents, approve of the action?); and (c) the ethical and legal status of any action that might be suggested by statistically significant results.

The third limitation is that statistical significance tests are designed to assess only sampling error (errors due to random sampling). More often than not, research published in academic journals is based on samples that are clearly not drawn at random (e.g., using students in a professor's class as research participants or using volunteers). Strictly speaking, there are no significance tests appropriate for testing differences when nonrandom samples are used. Nevertheless, quantitative researchers routinely apply significance tests to such samples. As a consequence, consumers of research should consider the results of such tests as providing only tenuous information.

Concluding Comment

Significance testing has an important role in quantitative research when differences are being assessed in light of sampling error (i.e., chance error). If researchers are trying to show that there is a real difference (when using random samples), their first hurdle is to use statistics (including the laws of probability) to show that the difference is statistically significant. If they pass this hurdle, they should then consider how large the difference is in absolute terms (e.g., 100 points on College Boards versus 10 points on College Boards). Then, they should evaluate the practical significance of the result. If they used nonrandom samples, any conclusions regarding significance (the first hurdle) should be considered highly tenuous.

Because many researchers are more highly trained in their content areas than in statistical methods, it is not surprising that some make the mistake of assuming that when they have statistically significant results, by definition they have important results and discuss their results accordingly. As a savvy consumer of research, you will know to consider the absolute size of any differences as well as the practical significance of the results when evaluating their research.

Notes

Appendix D

Checklist of Evaluation Questions

Following are the evaluation questions presented in Chapter 2 through Chapter 13 of this book. You may find it helpful to duplicate this appendix for use when evaluating research reports. Limited permission to do so is given on page *ii* of this book. Keep in mind that your professor may require you to justify each of your responses.

Chapter 2 Evaluating Titles

___ 1. Is the title sufficiently specific?

___ 2. Is the title reasonably concise?

___ 3. Are the primary variables referred to in the title?

___ 4. When there are many variables, are the *types* of variables referred to?

___ 5. Does the title identify the types of individuals who participated?

___ 6. If a study is strongly tied to a theory, is the name of the specific theory mentioned in the title?

___ 7. Has the author avoided describing results in the title?

___ 8. Has the author avoided using a "yes–no" question as a title?

___ 9. If there are a main title and a subtitle, do both provide important information about the research?

___ 10. If the title implies causality, does the method of research justify it?

___ 11. Is the title free of jargon and acronyms that might be unknown to the audience for the research report?

___ 12. Are any highly unique or very important characteristics of the study referred to in the title?

___ 13. Overall, is the title effective and appropriate?

Chapter 3 Evaluating Abstracts

___ 1. Is the purpose of the study referred to or at least clearly implied?

___ 2. Does the abstract mention highlights of the research methodology?

___ 3. Has the researcher omitted the titles of measures (except when these are the focus of the research)?

___ 4. Are the highlights of the results described?

___ 5. If the study is strongly tied to a theory, is the theory mentioned in the abstract?

___ 6. Has the researcher avoided making vague references to implications and future research directions?

___ 7. Overall, is the abstract effective and appropriate?

Chapter 4 Evaluating Introductions and Literature Reviews

___ 1. Does the researcher begin by identifying a specific problem area?

___ 2. Does the researcher establish the importance of the problem area?

___ 3. Are any underlying theories adequately described?

___ 4. Does the introduction move from topic to topic instead of from citation to citation?

___ 5. Are very long introductions broken into subsections, each with its own subheading?

___ 6. Has the researcher provided adequate conceptual definitions of key terms?

___ 7. Has the researcher cited sources for "factual" statements?

___ 8. Do the specific research purposes, questions, or hypotheses logically flow from the introductory material?

___ 9. Overall, is the introduction effective and appropriate?

Chapter 5 A Closer Look at Evaluating Literature Reviews

___ 1. Has the researcher avoided citing a large number of sources for a single point?

___ 2. Is the literature review critical?

___ 3. Is current research cited?

___ 4. Has the researcher distinguished between opinions and research findings?

___ 5. Has the researcher noted any gaps in the literature?

___ 6. Has the researcher interpreted research literature in light of the inherent limits of empirical research?

___ 7. Has the researcher avoided overuse of direct quotations from the literature?

___ 8. Overall, is the literature review portion of the introduction appropriate?

Chapter 6 Evaluating Samples When Researchers Generalize

___ 1. Was random sampling used?

___ 2. If random sampling was used, was it stratified?

___ 3. If some potential participants refused to participate, was the rate of participation reasonably high?

___ 4. If the response rate was low, did the researcher make multiple attempts to contact potential participants?

___ 5. Is there reason to believe that the participants and nonparticipants are similar on relevant variables?

___ 6. If a sample is not random, was it at least drawn from the target group for the generalization?

___ 7. If a sample is not random, was it drawn from diverse sources?

___ 8. If a sample is not random, does the researcher explicitly discuss this limitation?

___ 9. Has the author described relevant demographics of the sample?

___ 10. Is the overall size of the sample adequate?

___ 11. Is the number of participants in each subgroup sufficiently large?

___ 12. Has informed consent been obtained?

___ 13. Overall, is the sample appropriate for generalizing?

Chapter 7 Evaluating Samples When Researchers Do *Not* Generalize

___ 1. Has the researcher described the sample/population in sufficient detail?

___ 2. For a pilot study or developmental test of a theory, has the researcher used a sample with relevant demographics?

___ 3. Even if the purpose is not to generalize to a population, has the researcher used a sample of adequate size?

___ 4. Is the sample size adequate in terms of its orientation (quantitative versus qualitative)?

___ 5. If a purposive sample has been used, has the researcher indicated the basis for selecting participants?

___ 6. If a population has been studied, has it been clearly identified and described?

___ 7. Has informed consent been obtained?

___ 8. Overall, is the description of the sample adequate?

Chapter 8 Evaluating Measures

___ 1. Have the actual items and questions (or at least a sample of them) been provided?

___ 2. Are any specialized response formats, settings, and/or restrictions described in detail?

___ 3. When appropriate, were multiple methods used to collect data/information on each variable?

___ 4. For published measures, have sources been cited where additional information can be obtained?

___ 5. When delving into sensitive matters, is there reason to believe that accurate data were obtained?

___ 6. Have steps been taken to keep the measures from influencing any overt behaviors that were observed?

___ 7. If the collection and coding of observations involves subjectivity, is there evidence of interobserver reliability?

___ 8. If a measure is designed to measure a single unitary trait, does it have adequate internal consistency?

___ 9. For stable traits, is there evidence of temporal stability?

___ 10. When appropriate, is there evidence of content validity?

___ 11. When appropriate, is there evidence of empirical validity?

___ 12. Do the researchers discuss obvious limitations of their measures?

___ 13. Overall, are the measures adequate?

Chapter 9 Evaluating Experimental Procedures

___ 1. If two or more groups were compared, were the participants assigned at random to the groups?

___ 2. If two or more comparison groups were not formed at random, is there evidence that they were initially equal in important ways?

___ 3. If only a single participant or a single group is used, have the treatments been alternated?

___ 4. Are the treatments described in sufficient detail?

___ 5. If the treatments were administered by individuals other than the researcher, were those individuals properly trained?

___ 6. If the treatments were administered by individuals other than the researcher, were they monitored?

___ 7. If each treatment group had a different person administering a treatment, did the researcher try to eliminate the personal effect?

___ 8. If treatments were self-administered, did the researcher check on treatment compliance?

___ 9. Except for differences in the treatments, were all other conditions the same in the experimental and control groups?

___ 10. When appropriate, have the researchers considered possible demand characteristics?

___ 11. Is the setting for the experiment natural?

___ 12. Has the researcher distinguished between random selection and random assignment?

___ 13. Has the researcher considered attrition?

___ 14. Has the researcher used ethical and politically acceptable treatments?

___ 15. Overall, was the experiment properly conducted?

Chapter 10 Evaluating Analysis and Results Sections: Quantitative Research

___ 1. When percentages are reported, are the underlying numbers of cases also reported?

___ 2. Are means reported only for approximately symmetrical distributions?

___ 3. If any differences are statistically significant and small, have the researchers noted that they are small?

___ 4. Is the Results section a cohesive essay?

___ 5. Does the researcher refer back to the research hypotheses, purposes, or questions originally stated in the introduction?

___ 6. When there are a number of related statistics, have they been presented in a table?

___ 7. If there are tables, are their highlights discussed in the narrative of the Results section?

___ 8. Have the researchers presented descriptive statistics before presenting the results of inferential tests?

___ 9. Overall, is the presentation of the results comprehensible?

___ 10. Overall, is the presentation of the results adequate?

Chapter 11 Evaluating Analysis and Results Sections: Qualitative Research

___ 1. Were the data analyzed independently by two or more individuals?

___ 2. Did the researchers seek feedback from experienced individuals and auditors before finalizing the results?

___ 3. Did the researchers seek feedback from the participants (i.e., use member checking) before finalizing the results?

___ 4. Did the researchers name the method of analysis they used and provide a reference for it?

___ 5. Did the researchers state *specifically* how the method of analysis was applied?

___ 6. Did the researchers self-disclose their backgrounds?

___ 7. Are the results of qualitative studies adequately supported with examples of quotations or descriptions of observations?

___ 8. Are appropriate statistics reported (especially for demographics)?

___ 9. Overall, is the Results section clearly organized?

___ 10. Overall, is the presentation of the results adequate?

Chapter 12 Evaluating Discussion Sections

___ 1. In long articles, do the researchers briefly summarize the purpose and results at the beginning of the Discussion section?

___ 2. Do the researchers acknowledge specific methodological limitations?

___ 3. Are the results discussed in terms of the literature cited in the introduction?

___ 4. Have the researchers avoided citing new references in the Discussion section?

___ 5. Are specific implications discussed?

___ 6. Are the results discussed in terms of any relevant theories?

___ 7. Are suggestions for future research specific?

___ 8. Have the researchers distinguished between speculation and data-based conclusions?

___ 9. Overall, is the Discussion section effective and appropriate?

Chapter 13 Putting It All Together

___ 1. In your judgment, has the researcher selected an important problem?

___ 2. Were the researchers reflective?

___ 3. Is the report cohesive?

___ 4. Does the report extend the boundaries of the knowledge on a topic, especially for understanding relevant theories?

___ 5. Are any major methodological flaws unavoidable or forgivable?

___ 6. Is the research likely to inspire additional research?

___ 7. Is the research likely to help in decision making?

___ 8. All things considered, is the report worthy of publication in an academic journal?

___ 9. Would you be proud to have your name on the research article as a co-author?

Notes

Notes

Notes

Notes